The Windfall Club

What To Do When Life Deals You a Good Hand

Janne Ashton

Eloquent Books

Eloquent Books
An imprint of Strategic Book Group
P. O. Box 333
Durham, CT 06422
www.StrategicBookGroup.com

ISBN: 978-1-60860-330-5

Printed in the United States of America

Book Design: Judy Maenle

Author's note: There are quite a few technical terms used in this book. For this reason I have included a glossary at the end of the book. For any word in *italics* in this book, you will find its meaning in the glossary.

Important Notice: The purpose of this book is to provide education. All care has been taken to ensure that the information in this book is correct at the time of writing. It is, however, subject to change. It is important to obtain professional advice about your own situation before making any financial decisions.

About the Author

Janne Ashton was born and educated in Sydney, and started her working life as an economics teacher. She spent most of the next 20 years in various parts of the country. She was married and living on the mid north coast of New South Wales when her two children, Byron and Lee, were born. At that time, she was living in an unfinished house, with no electricity and no hot water. She describes her lifestyle at that time as "living in abject poverty."

When Byron was three and Lee was one, her marriage ended. She jokes that her son, Lee, walked one day, and her husband at the time walked the next day (he left the day after Lee took his first steps). This took her further into poverty. She then broke her leg and was unable to work for over two months. Following that, Janne's car broke down and needed major (and expensive) repairs to the motor. Janne can now confirm that she has tried poverty, and it is overrated.

Janne was determined to improve conditions for herself and her boys and, after 18 months of hard work and use of financial planning strategy, Janne managed to purchase a home for herself and her boys. This was "a move to another century."

This house was beautiful, had a huge spa, dishwasher, electric garage doors (a huge change after having no electricity for five years), a beautiful garden backing on to a reserve, as well as sweeping ocean views from all rooms, and a huge balcony overlooking the ocean. It was only a two-minute walk to the beach. From there, Janne worked part time as a self employed *financial planner*, so that she could spend time with her children whilst they were still at home. She went on to full time work once her younger son, Lee, started school.

Her job brought her many benefits, including her second husband, Garry, improved income and financial planning knowledge, much travel, and a move back to Sydney.

In 2004, Janne started her own financial planning business, Plan Protect, and was soon joined by her son, Byron, and shortly after by her husband, Garry. Her son, Lee, describes working in an office as "torture" although he has done the odd short stint at Plan Protect.

Janne started in financial planning when a number of people she knew received advice that she felt was inappropriate to their situation. She developed a true passion for it once she realised first hand the effect of having an injury with no income protection, and when she was able to use financial planning principles to turn her own lifestyle around.

She now lives on the northern beaches in Sydney with her husband, Garry, sons, Byron and Lee, Lee's girlfriend, Katie, and the family cat, Sid. Janne is a regular swimmer, and says that she lives in paradise.

Her business has brought her into contact with many people who have received a windfall. She believes that there are two defining factors in determining who is able to correctly manage the money, and thereby keep it. The first is education, and the second is appropriate advice. This book was written to give everyone access to information that can make a windfall last a lifetime, and longer.

Acknowledgements

As with all projects, this book was not completed by one person alone. There were many people who gave helpful advice and comments, after spending many hours reading and looking for ways to make this book more acceptable to you, the reader.

So please join me in thanking:

Tammy Logan, without whom this book would never have been written. Tammy gave me the idea to write the book, and helped with book structure and cast her expert technical eye over the book to ensure accuracy.

Annie Sassin, whose valuable comments, insight, and tact helped tremendously in making the book more readable.

Helen Shao, who shared her experience as an author (*Your First Home Made Easy*) to help me get to publishing stage.

John Dyall, from AXA Financial Planning, who composed the subtitle.

Byron Pritchard (my son), who helped with some great suggestions on content of the book.

Rob de Ridder, who is one of the few people who gets excited by tax, and helped with some of technical aspects of tax.

Adrian Lynch, who gave me the idea to include sportspeople and entertainers as windfall recipients.

My clients, many of whom are mentioned in the book (you know who you are), and without whom this book would have been less readable and less relevant. Thank you for making the profession of financial planning a pleasure rather than a job.

My staff at the time of writing: Anthony, Louise, Tammy, Pamela, William, Julian, and Byron, who look after me each day at work and who looked after my clients for me on days when I was at home finishing this book.

The dedicated staff at Strategic Book Group for their assistance and commitment throughout the publishing process.

My family, Garry, Byron, Lee, and Katie, and my friends, who encouraged me and never tried to talk me out of writing this book.

Table of Contents

CHAPTER 1

Introduction

*Look, if you had **one shot,** or **one opportunity***
*To seize everything you ever wanted-**One***
moment Would you capture it or just let it slip?

"Lose Yourself" by Marshall Mathers (Eminem)

It's what we all wish for, talk about, and dream about for most of our adult lives—a windfall of some sort—usually a lottery win or a large inheritance from a relative, often distant and not yet known. It may be the sale of a business, retirement, or other less yearned-for windfalls such as compensation claims, an inheritance from parents or loved ones, divorce, *redundancy* payments, or large insurance payouts. You may become a famous sports person or entertainer, and therefore need to manage sudden wealth.

Some of these windfalls may come at a high cost, but still provide material wealth that may not be expected by traditional methods of working hard and saving hard. In fact, this is the main attraction of a windfall; it is a large amount of money which arrives all at once and without the hard work or the time that is generally needed to accumulate wealth. Another characteristic of a windfall is that for most people it is irreplaceable. It is for this reason that it is so important that we treat a windfall with care.

Retirement and sale of a business are different from other windfalls in that there is hard work and time taken to put together a significant retirement benefit, or a profitable business. Sports people and entertainers fit into this category, as well. We may see them as "overnight successes," but there are years of hard work behind the scenes that is often forgotten. The reason I have included these as windfall events is that, for most people, it is the largest amount of money that they have had to handle up to that point. Also, in the case of retirement, there is usually no second chance to recoup the money, as your working life is over.

Divorce is rarely a windfall, but is included because it may result in one partner receiving a substantial *cash* payout, which needs to be closely managed. The same principles apply in this instance as in the case of true windfalls.

So how does this change the lives of those who come into this unexpected fortune? We hear lots of tales of doom and misery, which makes the rest of us feel better about the fact that we did not win that fortune. But how much is true, and do windfalls really make or break people's lives? Of course, the answer to this question varies. Those with education, advice and an awareness of both their own attitude to the windfall and the attitude of those around them are the ones who are most likely to have a long-term benefit from their sudden wealth.

In this book, we look at the issues facing those who have been fortunate enough to come into a large sum of money. We look at what often happens, how to avoid any pitfalls, and how to use the money to best advantage, regardless of your age, sex, goals, background, or experience with money. In this book are strategies that will ensure continued wealth over the long term, without the worry of "how long will it last?"

I have broken down the process of managing a windfall into three simple steps:

1. PREPARE
2. PLAN
3. REVIEW

Using these three simple steps will revolutionise the way you look at your finances. How are these three steps different from other books about money? I look at your emotional as well as your practical response to a windfall. This gives you insight into the subconscious way your mind works, and allows you to prepare, plan, and review your emotional reaction. This is complemented by simple and practical information that will help you in your decision making.

The Windfall Club is written for anyone who wants to learn to manage their money effectively, even if they have not yet had the windfall of their dreams. For those who have had a windfall, it is a "must read," and the best investment you can make before any other decisions are made.

Here is an education for everyone who wants to learn how to manage their financial decisions. This is a handbook for what to do and what not to do, when to make decisions and when to take a break from decision making, how to plan your future and where to get the best advice, how to avoid scams from both friends and strangers and, most of all, how your money can provide the wealth and happiness of your dreams.

You will learn about the various types of investments available, their strengths and weaknesses, when to use them, and when it is not appropriate. You will learn the tax consequences of your financial decisions, how to maximise the amount you leave to your *beneficiaries*, so that your windfall not only can look after you for the rest of your life, but also future generations.

There are many stories of clients and their windfall experiences. I have, of course, changed the names to protect their privacy. It is one of the best ways to learn, as we all relate to a real life experience.

Some of the information in this book is subject to change. Much of it is based on current tax and *superannuation* law. This can change overnight, so some of the information may go out of date. You can receive regular updates by becoming a member of the Windfall Club. This is free to join. Simply go to **www.thewindfallclub.com.au**. Please email me with your comments, tips, and feedback for future editions. Feel free to ask me any questions about the content of the book in your email. I would love to hear from you.

By becoming a member of the Windfall Club, you not only get free updates, but you also have ongoing support, in that you can email questions at any time, and I will happily provide answers to your questions. I will also give regular information by newsletter, on topics that are relevant to windfall recipients. You will also have the chance to network with other windfall recipients.

In the following chapters, we show you how you can protect yourself, your future, and your money, using education and advice. This book provides education that you can use on an ongoing basis. Refer to it regularly when you feel that you need a refresher course, and get regular advice from your professional team. This will keep you on track so that your windfall will provide you with a better lifestyle than you ever thought possible.

At the end of each chapter, there is a summary of the information in the chapter. You can use this as a short guide to what to do, after you have finished the book. You may find as you read more of this book that you feel you know enough. Keep going. Each chapter has been included for a very good reason—it is part of the education needed to ensure longevity of your windfall.

I hope you enjoy this book and find plenty of useful information. It is always fun to read about money, and how to make the most of it. So read on, and enjoy!

Phase One:
PREPARE

CHAPTER 2

The Emotional Reaction

"I'm gonna smile 'cause I deserve to."

"Better in Time" by Leona Lewis

It's an emotional time, hearing about a windfall, and the strength of the emotions will vary according to the amount involved (relative to your pre-windfall level of wealth), and the circumstances in which it is received. The nature of the individual will also play an important role, and this is something which you need to be aware of, and be prepared to manage.

Managing your emotions is one of the key skills required by a windfall recipient. It can also be one of the toughest. You are suddenly placed in a time of extreme emotion, caused by the receipt of the windfall (and/or the circumstances which brought about the windfall). So at the same time, extreme emotions become both the effect of the windfall, and the potential cause of its loss. No wonder so many windfalls are short-lived!

Now, let's look at the various windfalls that this book covers. I shall go on to cover the most common emotional reactions to a windfall, and then provide a strategy to allow rational (rather than emotional) decision making. This is an extremely important part of the book, as it is very easy to separate emotional decision makers from their money.

Retirement   This is usually a joyous time. I often ask my clients when they would like to retire, and I often get the answer "yesterday." Much of the wealth creation that we do during our lives—*superannuation*, investment property, shares, *managed* *funds*, and any other saving or investment—is used for setting us up so that we can live well without having to work.

There can, of course, be some negative emotions associated with retirement, especially if it is forced upon us by our employer, or ill health. Even if that is not the case, it is a time of change, and creates a void that needs to be filled. Many people take this in their stride, whilst others may find it difficult. Work does not just provide financial rewards, but also intellectual and social stimulation. It may also support our self esteem; many of us see ourselves as a successful teacher, builder, business person, etc. As well as filling much of the daylight (or night time) hours, it also gives structure and purpose to our day.

Many clients report that they are bored, lonely, or frustrated when they retire. I have known people who combat these emotions with "retail therapy." They shop 'til they drop, and this often ends in disaster, as they quickly run out of money.

Inheritance This comes with a completely different set of emotions from the lottery win. This is often accompanied by grief, as it is usually those closest to us who leave us significant amounts of money. Grief can be a debilitating emotion, and leaves us without the will to do anything much at all. It can also lead to a lack of responsiveness, where we are not interested in the money, as it came at such a price.

One of my clients, Maria, whose husband had died tragically in an accident, was not at all interested in the significant sum of money left to her through her husband's insurance. She just wanted her husband back. Six years later, she is still not interested in the money, and although it has been invested and made good returns, she has never asked how it is going, or shown any interest in it. I discuss it with her and her adult children together, and they are the ones who make the decisions as to what to do because, to her, the price was just too high.

Most people do get past this stage, particularly when the inheritance is from parents, whom we expect to outlive. Inheritances are left for us by those who love us, as they wish for us to have the benefit of their assets, so that we can improve our own lives.

Redundancy This can be either an exciting time or a time of emotional devastation. I worked in one of Australia's major banks when they went through a time of restructure. At the time, they were trying to change the focus of the bank from a service model to a sales model. This involved getting all the staff to see themselves as sales people, and to get them to actively sell to the clients. These people had been employed as service providers, and they were neither interested in nor suited to sales. Consequently, they suddenly found their jobs stressful and unenjoyable.

When the bank decided to make some people redundant, there was an overwhelming number of staff thinking, "Pick me." To those who had long years of service (many of them) this represented a windfall of note, and they were easily employable outside the bank.

About ten years later, the bank went through another restructure, and this also involved many redundancies. These were not wished for, and were in many cases given to people who were happy in their work. This brings up a whole new set of emotions. The obvious one is "why me" and, in many cases, the people who are picked are those who are seen to be achieving less than their peers.

There are exceptions, and the person who had been the best manager I had ever had was one of the ones to go. Of course, he was quickly snapped up by another major bank. For those who did not choose *redundancy*, and whose prospects of immediate employment are not high, this is a highly stressful time, and also a period where financial decisions are extremely relevant to future lifestyle.

Compensation Claim/Insurance Payout I have grouped these together as they both come about because of some sort of physical, mental or emotional trauma. These are often the most difficult to deal with, as the cost is one that most people would never willingly pay. If you ask anyone who has had a big payout under these conditions, they will nearly all say that they would willingly give up the money to get their health back. This, of course, is all the more reason to treat the money with respect, as it is all you do have to replace your health. Whilst it may be a poor substitute, it is a substitute that is generally needed to pay for ongoing medical help, and to compensate for your loss of health.

Anger is a common emotion felt in these circumstances, particularly in compensation cases. The anger can be directed at the cause of the problem, at yourself for putting yourself in danger, or just at the unfairness of it all, without directing it at any person or group. It may also be anger at the perceived small value of the payout, compared to the significance of the loss.

There is often fear of the future, and of how to cope with the mechanics of life, let alone trying to control a large sum of money that you may feel ill equipped to handle.

Divorce   I debated whether I would include divorce in a book about windfalls, as it is generally dividing the combined wealth of two people and using it to support two households instead of one. My usual comment about divorce is that it is a "wealth depletion strategy." This is certainly not most people's idea of a windfall.

I decided to include it, as it is a time when often a lump sum of cash is presented to one of the partners in the marriage, whilst the other may keep the physical assets. As this is also a difficult time emotionally, it presents a risk to the recipient of the money, in that they have to make decisions about the money at an extremely emotional and distressing time. As this book is about risk minimisation, I felt it should be included.

It is interesting to note that divorce is one of the reasons for Australia's ever increasing property prices, as the number of households in Australia have increased, not just because of population growth, but also because of increasing need for extra property created by divorce. This has therefore increased the demand for property, and so the price has risen.

Divorce is an emotional time for all of us, and many people experience a loss of wealth rather than a windfall. Emotionally, this can be a time of anger, loss, grief, fear of change (change is usually huge, and not limited to personal or financial), and often bitterness. I often described myself at this time as "a nervous breakdown walking around undiagnosed," and whilst this is an exaggeration, it is not too far from the truth. I don't think too many rational thoughts entered my head for around a year, and then I started to recognise my return to my old self.

This is not to say that we don't manage day-to-day life, and many do it extremely well. It is just that, for some of us, our thinking is tangled up in some very strong emotions, most of which are negative, and generally destructive to our self esteem.

Sale of Business This is unlike other windfalls, in that even though the receipt of the money is sudden, it is generally because of years of hard work beforehand. I have included it in this book because the many years of hard work have not necessarily produced a high level of income, as much is often reinvested into the business. Frequently the potential income from investing the proceeds of the sale of the business may be much greater than the income produced by the business itself.

This often also comes along with retirement or change of employment (unless you continue to work in your business for the new owner), so there are multiple stresses to deal with at once. When we recently bought a business, the previous owner (who continued to work in the business) was quite dismayed when he realised that he would need our permission to take holidays. He had been his own boss for 20 years, and this was the thing that brought home to him his new situation.

The main emotions to manage at this time are those associated with change. Most people dislike and, in fact, fear change. It is important to mitigate against the things you fear. It may be boredom, or fear of wealth in the form of money (you had the wealth before—it was just not so obvious whilst it was tied up in a business). It could possibly be the fear of starting your career all over again, particularly if a restraint of trade (this is when you agree not to be involved in a similar or competitive business for a period of time) has been agreed to with the purchaser.

Lottery Win   This is probably the most exciting of all windfalls, in that it is literally out of the blue. We all talk about what we would do if we won the lottery (even if we haven't bought the ticket) but we don't really expect to win. Our dreams about what we would buy are often not based on any sound thinking, and are generally just a wish list of all the things that seem impossible in our present circumstances.

One common theme is a list of people that we would give money to—as if we would become some benefactor to all and sundry, paying off mortgages, buying houses for people, and generally being the grand fixer of everyone's problems. Whilst this is commendable, it is rarely practical, as it is usually overstated compared to the size of the win.

The first emotion is generally overwhelming joy or exuberance at such an incredible win, which can often be followed by numbness—you're not sure what to feel! These emotions are clues to your subconscious mind's reaction to this windfall. Take time out to listen to your emotional responses and work out how you really feel about the money. I shall go through some of the more typical responses later in this chapter, and some effective methods to deal with them.

Sports People and Entertainers   For these people, fame and fortune generally come hand in hand, and whilst they have spent years perfecting their craft, the change from unknown to famous may often be sudden. In the case of a sports person, it may be getting into one of the top sporting teams, where games are televised and players become well known to the millions of viewers, or it may be that they have become highly ranked in their field.

Entertainers may achieve fame and fortune through a television show or movie, or by releasing a top selling album. You only need to watch reality TV show, *Australian Idol,* to see how people may quickly become household names, and go on to have a successful music career.

This is, of course, an exciting time, particularly as it coincides with public recognition of your achievements in your field. You are now considered an expert in your craft or sport and, at the same time, are earning a fortune. There are usually significant lifestyle changes that happen at this time. Often the "lifestyle of the rich and famous" goes with the territory, and there is a seemingly endless amount of cash available for spending. Money is easily spent on keeping up with other "rich and famous" people. Clothes, cars, holidays, and entertainment can quickly erode a fortune, with nothing much to show for it when the money runs out.

One of the main issues for entertainers and sports people is that the fortune may be short-lived. I was told yesterday that the average professional career of a footballer is about two and a half years. Actors, musicians, and other sports people are often in a similar situation. Sports people may only be able to stay in peak physical condition for a number of years, and then their body lets them down, either through injury or age. Whilst entertainers are less likely to have their careers ended in these ways, fashions and tastes may change, or they may choose a quieter lifestyle after a time.

Secondly, fame is almost always part of the mix for these people. Whilst this has its good points, and is often sought after, it often results in loss of privacy and an expectation that you must be beyond reproach. Entertainers and sports people are seen as role models for young people and, as such are criticised for things that the rest of us do without consequences. How often do you see pictures of a celebrity who has had too much to drink? Many of us have had occasions when we have drunk too much, but don't see photos of ourselves (looking our absolute worst) in a magazine the next week.

What an emotional rollercoaster this must be—fame, fortune, exciting lifestyle, loss of privacy, recognition, and, of course, all the people who become sudden friends, many with a specific agenda which allows them to benefit from your success. Frequently, the questions like "Why me?" or "Am I worthy?" will surface. There is a fine line between humility, which can keep you grounded, and self doubt, which can be destructive, both emotionally and financially.

EMOTIONAL RESPONSES

Below, I have listed the main emotions that will be experienced by a windfall recipient. The purpose of including these is so that you can recognise the emotions as they happen to you, as you are often unable to recognise them when you are in the depths of the emotion.

Joy   This is the typical emotion of lottery winners, sports people, and entertainers. Although this is a positive emotion, it is too extreme an emotion to promote rational decision making. Often with newfound wealth, it appears that you have an endless supply of money, and that caution and planning are unnecessary because of the magnitude of the sum of money. This, of course, is rarely the case.

People who are in the joy phase can be targets for scammers, and also well meaning but jealous family and friends. If you have won or earned over a million dollars, then a request for, say, $50,000 may seem small and not destructive to your financial position. Several requests for money from family and friends, however, can deplete the money very quickly. How often do you read about a famous pop star who has lost their millions, often at the hands of those they trusted?

I heard an interview on the radio a couple of years ago with someone who had won $1,000,000. When asked about the money, she replied, "Oh, that's gone." This was about two or three years after she had won the prize. From the rest of the interview, it was apparent that she was not financially better off than before. That is fine, if that was her plan, but with most people, they don't plan to fail; they just fail to plan.

Grief   This is usually an emotion that is brought on by loss. We usually associate grief with the loss of a loved one, and that is easy to recognise. Grief, however, can also be brought on by the loss of a job or business, a loss of good health, or divorce. In her book titled *On Death and Dying*, Elisabeth Kubler-Ross describes five stages of grief: denial, anger, bargaining, depression, and acceptance. Whilst not everyone goes through all these stages, she believes that everyone goes through at least two. These stages apply to grief, regardless of the cause.

For example, in the case of redundancy, the process may be something like this. Denial: "You're joking; you can't do this to me. I have a family to look after." Anger: "That company/boss is so ruthless! How dare they make me redundant!" Bargaining: "Maybe they can find another position for me." Depression: "I'm obviously no good; that's why they got rid of me." Acceptance: "Well, there is probably something better out there; I just have to find it."

Clearly, the first four stages are not the time to make a decision, as your emotions are putting you through a hard time. The acceptance stage is the first positive emotion that you have felt during this process, and once you have entered that stage, you are more ready to make a decision.

Fear/Fear of Loss   A large amount of money brings along with it lots of responsibility. There are decisions to be made, lots of discussions with advisers, tax to be paid, and, often, a more complex financial structure than before. This can be overwhelming, particularly to someone who is used to a more simple structure. Many clients express a fear of losing the money, or a fear of not being able to handle the decision making process, and they may fear their friends' and family's reaction to their sudden wealth.

The role of the *financial planner* is crucial, as this is the professional that is there to guide you through this time. Fear can be a paralysing emotion, and this can render decision making almost impossible. Once the fear is recognised, it can be addressed. The more you know about something, the less frightening it becomes.

Remember when you first learned to drive? Even turning a corner was scary! The more you learnt about driving, the more relaxed you became. It is the same with money. The more you know about it, the easier it is. Read whatever you can that helps you understand that which you fear, and discuss this emotion with your financial planner. The more the planner knows about what you are going through, the more help s/he can provide. Education is your best weapon against fear, and this book is just that—an education for the newly wealthy.

Guilt   This often comes along with an inheritance. You may feel that here are you with your sudden wealth, and you should not be enjoying it because someone you love had to die for you to receive the money. This is a gift from them to you, and gifts are meant to be enjoyed by the recipient. Guilt, along with most other extreme emotional responses, can cause poor decision making. It is closely related to grief, and it is important to work through it before too many choices are made about your future.

Numbness   This is often a form of shock, protecting you from a rush of emotions that may be too much to handle. As the numbness disappears, it will be replaced by a number of emotions, (probably at least some of those mentioned above) which can then be dealt with in an appropriate way.

Boredom   Those who stop work after a windfall may start to feel bored. It sounds great, never having to work again, but it can cause a whole new set of problems. There is a limit to the amount of holidays and shopping that you can find fulfilling and, even if that is not the case, you may find that your windfall diminishes rapidly. Boredom comes about because of lack of planning. I don't mean you have to plan every minute of the day, but giving up one thing means replacing it with something else that is affordable on your budget.

Depression   This is one of the most common "diseases" of modern times. So many people find day-to-day life difficult, even without any obvious cause. While a windfall does not appear to be a likely cause, it can be as it can take away our goals (if we let it). Think of all the things we strive for, and this gives both focus and activity to our days. Suddenly, we may feel that there is no longer a need to strive as we have the ability to get whatever we want. We also have lost the commonality with a lot of our friends, who are still where we were in pre-windfall times.

To me, the best antidote for depression is to have a goal, and involve yourself in working towards that goal. While windfall recipients may feel that they no longer need goals, this is simply not the case. You may need to think of an entirely different set of goals, which may not be related to financial freedom, as this may have already been achieved. Certainly, getting an appropriate education to manage your windfall effectively is a goal that should not be neglected.

Frustration The main cause of frustration for windfall recipients is that they are often surprised that they still have issues to deal with, when they thought that the money would solve everything. I have had clients say to me, "Sometimes I think it is more trouble than it's worth." This is simply a reaction to change, and will quickly pass once your plan is in place. You may also be frustrated with the reaction of others, as it may cause some tension in some of your relationships.

Low Self Esteem Although this is not an emotional reaction to a windfall, this is addressed because it is often the thing that makes us get rid of the money. A poor self image is a subconscious belief that we are not a worthy person. The unworthiness may relate to a particular area of our lives (we may feel unworthy of, say, wealth) or it may be a general feeling. Either way, if we feel unworthy, we will go through a process of getting rid of the money, as we believe we don't deserve it. Although a professional or close friend or family member may recognise this in you, it is much harder to halt the process.

I have a client who often talks about a family member who is "unlucky." The fact is that, because of her low self esteem, she consistently makes poor choices in her life. If you feel that this is relevant to you, you may wish to enrol in a Neuro-Linguistic Programming (NLP) course, or speak to a psychologist about this aspect of yourself. These may help you to improve your self image, thereby resulting in better decision making.

Effective Strategies   In this highly emotional time, you need to find a way to cope with both the rush of feelings and the sudden wealth. The strategies below are all designed to minimise the risk to you, not only of losing the money, but also the risk of emotional fallout which can include breakdown in relationships and loss of confidence that can occur at these times.

1. **Tell No one.**   This is one of the best strategies when you first receive a windfall. In the case of sports people and entertainers, everyone knows when you are earning a fortune, so this tactic is not available to you, but the other strategies in this book will work for you.

   Most people, even those closest to you, will feel jealous, and this can be shown in a number of ways. Rarely will they come out and say it. They will use different tactics to make themselves feel better. The most common one is to ask you for some of the money; not straight away, but very shortly afterwards. This will "even the score" somewhat. Their reactions will come tied up in some emotional blackmail, and may sound something like:

   • I really need this money or . . . (something terrible will happen).
   • You know I wouldn't ask you if I didn't really need it.
   • This is my big chance.
   • You know I would do it for you (if I had the money).
   • I have this great business opportunity.
   • I need an investor for this great business opportunity (you will make a fortune).
   • If only I had . . . (something that costs lots of money).

   If you have already told some of your family, friends, or work colleagues, don't worry about it. Just be prepared to follow the instructions below, and these will give you a path to follow which will take most of the awkwardness out of the situations described above.

   One of my clients, Teresa, won a small amount of money in a competition. She didn't tell her family, but used some of the money to buy things for them that made their lives easier.

She was generous and thoughtful. Her silence about this comparatively small windfall ($50,000) was a great strategy. It took away any expectations from her family, and allowed her to choose a level of generosity that worked for her, and was a lovely surprise for her adult children, who never knew of her windfall.

2. **Say NO** There is a simple way of dealing with requests for money—say **NO**. This may sound easy, but it is not. It is, though, a whole lot easier than losing all the money. A simple, "I haven't made any decision yet as to what I'm doing," or, "I would just like to get some advice first before I make any decisions" will defer the decision until you have had time to get over the rush of emotions and get advice to determine what you need for yourself. Remember, it is your money, and you need to look after yourself first. If you have ever flown, you will notice that you are instructed to fit your own breathing apparatus first before helping others, including small children. There is a very good reason for this. It is only once you have protected yourself that you are in a position to help others. You cannot help others if you don't survive. This is the same with a windfall. You cannot help those you love if you do not survive financially. Below is a story of someone who didn't say no.

> *"Winning the lottery isn't always what it's cracked up to be," says Evelyn Adams, who won the New Jersey lottery, not just once, but twice (1985, 1986), to the tune of $5.4 million. Today the money is all gone and Adams lives in a trailer.*
>
> *"I won the American dream but I lost it, too. It was a very hard fall. It's called rock bottom," says Adams.*
>
> *"Everybody wanted my money. Everybody had their hand out. I never learned one simple word in the English language: 'No.' I wish I had the chance to do it all over again."*
>
> Source: "8 lottery winners who lost their millions," Ellen Goodstein, www.Bankrate.com

3. **Take Time**   Let yourself feel your responses. A windfall, by its very nature, is big. It has the capacity to make massive changes to your life; either good or bad. The saying "money is the root of all evil" has some basis in fact, as does the feeling that "everything would be all right if I just had more money." Money is neither good nor bad; it is a measure of value and the basis for all trade. There are just good decisions and bad decisions.

   Bad decisions are generally made during times of high emotion. Take the time to work through your emotions, and enjoy those that are pleasant. There is no set rule as to how long it will take to get through this period, and if you are aware that you are going through an emotional time, you are more likely to be aware of when your feelings are becoming more moderate.

4. **Educate Yourself**   Educating yourself on managing your emotions is the best way to manage risk, while at the same time adjusting to your new financial position. This is something worthwhile to do while you are in the "take time' phase. It does not involve decision-making, but does prepare you effectively for your new life. Read as much as you can about money. There are financial newspapers and magazines, books, articles on the internet, and courses available. Do not get your education from family or friends (unless they are finance professionals), as their view directly relates to their experience. I hear so many people say something like "I would never invest in that. Uncle John lost money doing that." Other people's bad experiences are often caused by poor planning. They are not necessarily relevant to you. Please see the end of the book for details on our courses, which are specifically designed to provide you with an effective education on managing your emotions and your money.

5. **Park Your Money**   There are plenty of bank accounts that will give you reasonable rates of interest while you park your money. Taking time out will also give you an honest but

reasonable answer to any requests for money from family and friends. "I am not making any decisions at the moment. I have put the money in an account and will seek advice from professionals so that I can evaluate my situation. So, I'm sorry, but at this stage I am unable to help."

6. **Obtain Advice**   Even if you want to help, don't do it without a *financial plan* in place. After the initial stress has started to subside, it is time to start planning your future. You will need a team of professionals, including a financial planner, an accountant, a solicitor, and possibly a mortgage broker and general insurance broker. No commitments are required at this point, just some careful soul searching, education, and planning.

It is extremely important that you are advised by the right professional. Many people feel that the best professional to go to for financial advice is an accountant. This is simply not the case, as it is illegal in Australia for an accountant (or anyone else) to give personal financial advice. This can only be given by a licensed financial planner. Conversely, financial planners cannot give tax advice, although thay can advise you on the tax consequences of financial decisions. Of course financial planners and accountants cannot give legal advice, and it is for this reason that you will need your professional team to work together. This can be co-ordinated by your financial planner.

7. **Finish Reading This Book**   You may feel that you are well equipped to know what to do now that you have completed this chapter. This is a start, and the rest of the book gives you a lot more information that is absolutely necessary to your financial education. Even if you know a bit about money, read on. There will certainly be some information in this book which will help you manage your money. The contents of *The Windfall Club* are designed to equip you with much of the education necessary for you now. Further information, updates, courses, and networking are available on the website, www.thewindfallclub.com.au

8. **Network With Other Windfall Recipients** One of the main issues for many windfall recipients is that they have no network of people in the same situation. People feel happier when they can network with others in a similar position, hence sporting clubs, business networking groups, play groups, social clubs, and any other group that draws like-minded people together.

Without a network, there can be a degree of isolation. Although you may have a large social network, it is difficult and often considered bad taste to discuss the issues caused by a large amount of money. How do you find other lottery winners, people with large inheritances, or those with a large insurance payout? Of course, it is possible, but for many windfall recipients, it just doesn't happen. Sports people are the exception here, as most of them operate within a team environment, and this has the advantage of providing a ready-made network of people in a similar situation.

The other advantage of networking with other windfall recipients is that they are less likely to be jealous of you, as they have their own windfall. Jealousy is a normal human emotion, and it is difficult to find someone who is not affected by it in some way, unless, of course, they are in the same situation as you.

I have addressed this issue with the title of both the book and the website. The Windfall Club is intended to be just that, a club for windfall recipients. The website provides free membership to the Windfall Club. You will be able to network with others in Windfall Club courses and social functions.

SUMMARY

When you first receive your windfall, you will have a rush of emotions. Some will be positive emotions, such as joy, whilst others may be negative, such as fear. Whatever the emotion, it will take away rational decision making, so this is not a time to make decisions.

By following eight simple steps, you will get through this initial period without placing your windfall at risk. The steps are:

1. Tell no one, but if you already have, see below.

2. Say **NO** to any requests for money.

3. Take time to get through your highly emotional time. Do **not** make any decisions whilst you are in this phase.

4. Educate yourself using this book, other books on money, financial newspapers and magazines, articles on the internet, and financial courses.

5. Obtain advice from professionals. You will need a financial planner, an accountant, a solicitor, and possibly a mortgage broker and general insurance broker.

6. Park your money in a bank account while you get through the emotional time, and until you have had advice from your professional team.

7. Finish reading this book before you do anything, as it is a complete set of instructions for you.

8. Network with other windfall recipients.

The next chapter will show you how to make the daunting task of managing your money seem easy, and give you the steps to follow so that you get exactly what you want from your money.

CHAPTER 3

Where Do I Go
for Advice?

*That's **why** we **seize** the **moment** try to freeze
it and own it, squeeze it and hold it Cause we
consider these minutes golden.*

*"Sing for the Moment" by
Marshall Mathers (Eminem)*

This is the most important phase in the process of becoming
a successful member of the Windfall Club. Skip this period
and you are likely to end up no better off than you were before.
These minutes truly are golden. They will set you up for a life
of successful investing, and a life filled with pleasures that only
money can buy. Managing money takes skill, time, patience,
education, professional advice, and a mind with purpose. There
are a number of questions you need to answer before you can
even begin to think about which investments are appropriate
for you.

Pick Your Team   This may sound daunting, but should not present a problem if you follow a logical method. You will require a
financial planner, an accountant, and a solicitor, preferably one
who has a sound knowledge of *estate planning*.

A few financial planning practices have an estate planning
and/or tax specialist, and this is very helpful if you can have
your team in one office. You will still need an accountant and
solicitor to implement the strategy recommended by the financial planning team. You may also need a mortgage broker and a

general insurance broker, and this can be determined during the planning stage.

Some financial planners work in teams with accountants and solicitors, or you can find your own team. Many people like to work with professionals who have been referred to them. I have clients, Alex and Ruby, who wouldn't see a financial planner because they were reluctant to disclose their situation to a stranger. They were struggling financially and felt that their only option was to sell their house. A trusted friend referred them to me, and their financial problem was easily fixed, without the need to sell the house.

If you don't know a financial planner, or if you haven't been referred to one by a friend or family member, you will need to find one using another method. There are financial planners in banks, and most large *financial institutions* have licensed financial planners. Financial planners can be found using the Financial Planning Association (FPA) or through the Australian Securities and Investments Commission (ASIC). Google and other internet search engines are another way to locate financial planners in your area.

Whichever method you use to find a financial planner, you will need to interview your prospect to see if the planner is suitable to your needs. There are a number of questions that you will need to ask to see if this person is someone you feel comfortable working with to achieve your financial goals. The following is a list of questions that you may wish to ask:

- How long have you been a financial planner?
- How many planners do you employ, and what is their experience in financial planning?
- What emphasis do you place on education, for both planners and *paraplanners*? (Paraplanners are the people who put together the financial plan and do the research necessary to ensure the financial plan is appropriate. This is done under the guidance of the financial planner, and, often, the paraplanner is the technical expert in the planning office.)
- What is your knowledge of my situation (windfall recipient) and how have you helped other windfall recipients?

- How long has your business been in operation, and will it continue to operate if you decide to retire, become ill, or have some other reason to stop work?
- How do you charge for your services, and do I have a choice as to how I pay you: commission, fee for service, or fee based (this can be a mix of commission and fees, where the planner will charge a fee, and offset this against commission)?
- How often will you update me on my financial position, and how will I pay for my reviews?
- Do you have a website that gives me access to my *portfolio*, as well as market updates and other information about financial products?
- Do you have a team that can provide support for me even if you are away from work?
- What differentiates you from other financial planners?
- Do you support any charities, so that some of my fees go to looking after those less fortunate?
- Are you happy to work together with my accountant and solicitor to ensure the correct implementation of my plan?

When you have interviewed some financial planners, it will become obvious to you who you wish to work with, and who impressed you the most. You will need to notice not just the answers to your questions, but also the attitude and interest of the planner in helping you. Someone who has a genuine interest in you will not need to tell you about him/herself (other than answering your questions)—s/he will be more interested in finding out about you.

Once you have chosen your financial planner, you will need to find an accountant and a solicitor. This may be arranged by your planner, or you can arrange it yourself.

If you already have a relationship with these professionals and you feel that they are equipped to handle your new situation, then that is fine. It is preferable to discuss with them your newfound wealth, and ask them if they are in a position to look after you. It is important that you have a team of professionals who are prepared to work together to give you the best result, as this ensures that all aspects of your finances are consolidated to achieve your goals.

WHAT INFORMATION WILL MY PLANNER NEED?

When you have your first meeting with your planner, you will probably talk about yourself more than you ever have before. S/he will ask you an amazing number of questions about anything which may be relevant to your financial needs. Financial planners need to have a complete picture of your situation so that they can give appropriate advice. My clients really enjoy this process, as it clarifies their position for them, and usually they have not done this themselves. Below, I have outlined the topics for discussion in your first interview.

Personal Details   These include name, date of birth, place of birth, marital status, children's details (if applicable), and contact details.

What Is Important to You?   This is a very personal part of your planning and one that forms the basis of your advice. Whether you are single, married, or in a personal relationship where the money will be jointly owned, you need to work out what your core values are. This is a major influence on what your decisions will be. What are the things that you are not prepared to compromise? Is it the house you want, children's education, a particular lifestyle, a level of income, or a level of gifting to others: friends, family, or charity.

Decide not only what, but who, is most important to you. This is relevant for lottery winners and sounds easy, but if you are beset by requests for money, then you may need to draw a line on your list and anyone below the line misses out. This is not the time to decide that, but it is good to have the list in place. Look back on your life, and realise that many friends come and go, and those who are important now may be mere acquaintances in a year's time.

Beware of anyone who suddenly becomes friendlier after the windfall, and of any recently formed friendships. These may become long term relationships, but are yet to stand the test of time. Sudden friends who are friendlier after news of your windfall may place you at risk, and are to be treated with extreme caution.

You will need to have your goals fairly clear in your mind before you see a financial planner, as this is generally one of the first questions they will ask in relation to your plan. A planner bases the financial plan on your goals. That way, it is relevant to what you wish to achieve. A financial plan takes you from where you are now to where you wish to be in the future; without goals, there can be no recommendation.

Your goals need to be specific, and may be short, medium, and long term. They do not need to necessarily be financial goals (an income of $100,000 per annum is an example of a financial goal). The goal may be that you want to start a family in two years' time. We call this a lifestyle goal. Whilst this is not a financial goal, it is very relevant to your financial plan, as it will cost money.

When discussing time frames, we generally class up to three years as short term, three to five years as medium term, and over five years as long term. These are related to investment time frames. Say, for example, that you wanted to spend some of your money in two years' time. Your windfall should not be invested in shares or property, as these can fluctuate in value in the short to medium term, and you could end up losing money. If, however, you wanted to spend that portion of the money in ten years, then shares and property may well be appropriate investments for you. We will discuss investments in greater detail in a later chapter.

A good financial planner will spend much of the first interview discussing your goals. Many of my clients say to me that they would like to be "well-off" in retirement. This may be very clear to them, and to me it may mean something else entirely. I had a very wealthy client, Sarah, who when asked what she needed to live on, replied that $300,000 would be sufficient. I came back to her with my recommendations and she was horrified because I had not arranged sufficient income for her, as much of it was reinvested. When I discussed with her that she had said she only needed $300,000, she replied "I need that each month!"

A client's idea of a good retirement becomes a talking point. We discuss holidays, entertaining, going out, golf, other sports, and gifts to children. We also discuss whether they will move to a new residence, or another town or city, and if they feel that they will spend more or less than they do whilst they are working. The answers are never the same from one client (or couple) to the next.

Your planner will work through each of your goals with you, and ask you to be quite specific about each one. This will give them sufficient information to fairly accurately assess the cost of fulfilling your dreams. They will at the same time allow for a buffer, as this will look after you if the cost estimates were a little low.

Once the goals and their order of importance have been established, your financial planner will then work with you to assess whether there are sufficient funds to achieve everything on the list. This is when it will become clear to you which goals must be included, and which ones are not essential. You may be able to include everything, but at a reduced amount.

For example, you may wish to take two holidays a year, costing $10,000 each. If the budget only allows for $15,000 to be spent on holidays, then you can still go on two holidays and spend less on each one, or have one holiday as planned, and one on a lower budget. This could be cheaper accommodation, shorter duration, or closer to home, thereby reducing the travel costs. Or, you could have one extra-special or extra-long holiday. Sometimes, you will need to delete (at least for the time being) some of the items on your list.

New clients, Peter and Susan, came to see me a few years ago and asked why they were in trouble financially. After doing a budget analysis, it was fairly clear that their expenses were greater than their income. They had two options: they could sell their house, or put their children into a public school rather than the private school they were attending.

They did not want to sell their house, but when I suggested educating their children at a public school, that was not an option. After much discussion (my advice would have been to keep the house, had this been acceptable to them), it was determined that the house had to go, as their children's schooling was their top priority.

Budgeting You will need to have some idea of what you currently spend, and what you intend to spend now that you have had a windfall. This is part of the plan, and it is important to have an accurate idea of both one-off expenses and ongoing spending. Budgets may be difficult for windfall recipients, and this is discussed at length in Chapter 10.

Employment If you are still working, your occupation, employer, salary, fringe benefits, hours of work, and any other relevant details will all need to be discussed.

Assets When you first visit your planner, you will need to give them a list of all your assets. You will need to include whatever you own from the following list:

- home
- contents
- vehicles
- bank accounts
- investments e.g. shares and property
- superannuation and pensions
- business assets and sale value of business
- family companies and trusts
- anything else that is not included above

Your planner will want details of each of these. It is best to bring a statement for any investments or superannuation if you have one. Copies of accounts for trusts and companies, as well as personal tax returns and pay slips are also good to have on hand to discuss with your planner.

Liabilities Most people have debt at some point during their working lives. Your financial planner will need to know the details of any debts you have, including the lender, the interest rate, whether the interest is fixed or variable, the term of the loan, and the repayment frequency and amount. Most of this information will be on your loan statement.

Superannuation and Pension Please bring in anything that you have that is relevant to existing superannuation or pensions. It is extremely important that your planner is aware of the full extent of any retirement planning that you have undertaken so far.

Insurance You will be asked for details of any insurance you have. These include any personal insurances (life, total and permanent disability, income protection, business overheads, trauma insurance) as well as your general insurances: health, home and contents, car, and any others.

Estate Planning Do you have a will? And if so, when was it last reviewed? Does anyone have a power of attorney for you? These are all questions that will need to be answered in your first interview with your planner. If you do have a will and/or a power of attorney, it is good to bring these documents with you to the meeting.

Risk Assessment This is a part of financial planning, which is essential in making the recommendations appropriate for you. Each person can have a different tolerance to *risk*. In financial planning, we describe risk as the possibility of investments falling in value over the short or medium term. For example, a *term deposit*, whilst generally not actually guaranteed, has virtually no chance of falling in value, and is therefore seen as a "safe" investment. At the time of writing (2009), the government is guaranteeing bank deposits. This was done to support the banking system during tough times.

An investment in, say, property, has the risk of falling in value in the short or medium term, and so this would not suit someone with a short investment term, or who was concerned about any falls in value of their assets.

Back in 1987, when the *sharemarket* was producing fabulous returns, I heard the following story. Jack had just sold his house and paid out the mortgage, and had $80,000 left. He decided to put it into the sharemarket whilst he looked for another house to buy. Before he found another house, the 1987 crash occurred, and his money fell in value to $30,000. I never heard the end of the story, whether he pulled his money out for a house or left it in shares. Either way, he would have been worse off, as property prices in Australia rose dramatically, because people left the sharemarket to invest in property. This is a classic case of a short term investor using the wrong investment. He should have invested his money in cash, and cash only.

Risk tolerance has two elements to it: time and personal choice. Your investment time frame must always be the first consideration. *Growth investments* (shares and property) are inappropriate for short or medium term investors. I am tempted to repeat the last sentence, as it is one of the most important sentences in the book.

So, here it is again: growth investments (shares and property) are inappropriate for short or medium term investors. Why is this so important? If you make decisions whilst you are in a period of emotional turmoil, you are likely to change your mind about what you want. This is often the key to lost fortunes.

I have a client, Priscilla, who invested her windfall in 2001, into managed funds (many of which invested in shares). The sharemarket fell and so did the value of her investments. She would ring me every so often and say, "Janne, I've had enough. I'm pulling out." I would talk her out of it by going through the original discussion about *volatility* (rises and falls in value of investment assets) and time frame, and explaining that in time, all would be well. We had some close calls and, to her credit, she stuck it out, and eventually had an excellent return on her investment.

Had she pulled out when her investment had fallen about 30 percent in value, she could not have recovered the money, as she was drawing more than what a "safe" investment would have paid her, so she would have been losing money every month. One of the reasons she wanted to withdraw the money was that she was constantly being told by family and friends that she had made a bad decision. I am sure that they were well meaning, but they did not help. All she had to do was stick to the timeframe (5+ years) and her investment was in great shape.

The second element to risk profiling is personal choice. We all have our own particular tolerance to risk, and a planner will complete a risk questionnaire to assess your particular preference. After assessing your time frame(s), the risk questionnaire will ask you the following types of questions:

- What is your investment experience?
- How would you rank your preference between high risk/ high growth and low risk/low growth investments?
- What would you do in the event of a market downturn?
- What is the relative importance of income and growth?
- What sort of return do you expect relative to *inflation* (this is known as the *"real"* rate of return, as any return up to the inflation rate is not improving your real position)?
- Do you have a preference for ethical investments?

All commonly-used questionnaires will have a number of pre-selected answers to choose from, which will give typical answers for each *risk profile*. This makes them easy for you to complete, as there will be one answer which will resonate with you more than the others.

The result of this exercise will be that the planner now has an idea of the style of investments that will suit you. This will be a mix of the various *asset classes* (cash, fixed interest, property, Australian shares, and international shares). Of course, not all asset classes are represented in each risk profile, and your particular blend of investments may have only two or three of the above choices. There are also investments that fall outside the main asset classes, and your planner may discuss these with you if s/he feels they are suitable for your particular situation. I shall discuss all the main areas of investment in Chapter 5.

The graph below shows typical growth of diversified funds over a 20 year period.

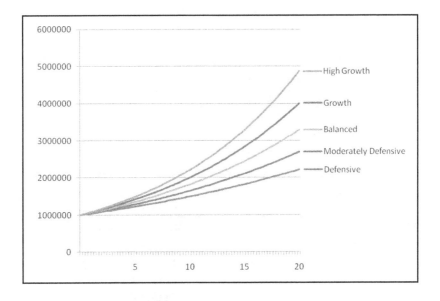

There are six common risk profiles that a planner may select for you, based on your responses to the questions in the risk questionnaire. These are designed to give you an appropriate spread of asset classes to match your personal choice. I have shown these in the table on the next page. Please note that the prime objective is the expected investment return expressed as a return in excess of inflation as measured by the *Consumer Price Index (CPI)*.

Janne Ashton

RISK PROFILE ASSESSMENT

Profile	Description of investor and investment
Cash	• Investment held in cash or cash based securities. Interest rates may vary. • Prime objective: CPI
Defensive	• Definite need for a very secure income. Little fluctuations in capital value. • Will not accept much downside risk. • Prime objective: CPI plus 1%
Moderately defensive	• Requires a stable income. Can withdraw capital to supplement income if necessary. • Expects small fluctuations in income to gain modest capital growth. • Requires minimisation of downside risk. • Prime objective: CPI plus 2%
Balanced	• Desires a reasonably stable income stream, but also desires a steady growth in capital value. • Prepared for fluctuations to achieve reasonable capital growth over the medium term. • Sufficient capital available to draw down to supplement income needs. • Prime objective: CPI plus 3%
Growth	• Little or no need for an ongoing current income from investments. • Investment focus is on achieving capital growth with no need to access capital in the medium term. • Prepared to accept fluctuations in capital value to achieve longer term wealth accumulation. • Prime objective: CPI plus 4%
High growth	• No ongoing income needed from investments. • Investment focus is on high levels of capital growth with no need to access capital for the long term. • Prepared to accept wide fluctuations in capital value and may be prepared to invest additional sums during downsize period. • Prime objective: CPI plus 5%

Source: AXA Financial Planning

As the risk profiles change from cash through to high growth, there is a greater exposure to growth assets (shares and property). Notice how the more you have in growth assets, the higher your average return will be. High growth investors will earn on average an extra 4 percent per annum (compared to a defensive investor) as a reward for putting up with that annoying volatility! So, how much difference will that extra 4 percent per annum make? Is it all worth it? The table below shows the value of $1,000,000 invested over periods of 5, 10, 15, and 20 years. I have assumed CPI (Consumer Price Index) at 3 percent, so returns are based on the above targeted returns (shown as prime objective).

RETURNS FOR DIFFERENT RISK PROFILES

	Defensive	Moderately Defensive	Balanced	Growth	High Growth
5 Years	$1,220,190	$1,282,037	$1,346,855	$1,414,778	$1,485,947
10 Years	$1,488,864	$1,643,619	$1,814,018	$2,001,597	$2,208,040
15 Years	$1,816,697	$2,107,181	$2,443,220	$2,831,816	$3,281,031
20 Years	$2,216,715	$2,701,485	$3,290,663	$4,006,392	$4,875,439

Notice that over a 5 year period, each extra percentage point adds over $60,000 to your total investment value. At 10 years, it has increased to over $150,000; at 15 years, a mere 1 percent adds about $300,000, and at 20 years, it is up to $500,000! This is achieved by just moving up one risk profile, say, from "moderately defensive" to "balanced." Over 20 years, the difference between "defensive" and "high growth" is a huge $2,600,000, or 260% extra return!

Of course, this is not to say that we all should be "high growth" investors. The risk with investing in a high risk profile is that, if you are not comfortable with volatility, you are likely to pull out in the tough times (when sharemarkets fall) and then have low returns, or even a *capital* loss. On the other hand, people who are too conservatively invested will over time receive a

Janne Ashton

lower rate of return than what would be available to them from their correct asset allocation.

What you need to do is ensure that you are invested appropriately for you.

In the case of a couple, each person may have a different risk profile. There are two schools of thought on how to handle this. The first says that you can blend the risk profiles, thereby averaging the investment styles of the two partners. To me, this is like saying that if you have your head in the oven and your feet in the freezer, on average, you are comfortable! I always recommend that, in this situation, you have separate investments for each partner which reflect their personal preference.

Once this has all been established, there will be a few things to sign to give the planner authority to research and complete the *Statement of Advice (S.O.A.)*. This can take some weeks, as there is a lot of work that goes into plan preparation, and there may well be plans ahead of yours in the queue. If anything comes to mind during the plan preparation phase that is relevant to what you want and has not already been discussed, it is important that you contact your adviser to work through any potential changes to your advice.

SUMMARY

- Pick your team. You will need a financial planner, a solicitor, an accountant, and possibly a general insurance broker and mortgage broker.
- Work out what is important to you. This will help you define your goals and also prioritise what you most want to achieve.
- Bring details of your income, assets, liabilities, insurance, budget, estate planning, superannuation, and employment to your first interview with your planner. The more detail the planner has, the better the plan.
- Your risk profile will determine the style of investments that the planner recommends.

You have now completed the "Prepare" phase and are now ready to enter the next phase: "Plan." Your planner will put together a plan which will be designed uniquely for you. Plans are often like a mini book just about you. There is a lot of information, some of which may be quite new to you. In the "Plan" section of this book, I go through the various topics covered by the plan, and give you some background information, so that you can easily understand what is being recommended, and why.

Phase Two:
PLAN

CHAPTER 4

The Financial Plan

Your financial plan is like an instruction book on how to get from where you are now (your current situation) to where you want to be in the future (goals). With your new windfall, you may not have to wait to get what you want, so the plan will provide the method that can be used to ensure that you can continue the lifestyle you want, not just now, but in the future as well.

It is simply like getting directions on a map. You need to find where you are now, and where you want to get to, and then the map will give you the directions. Of course, a financial plan is much more complex, as there are many things which can change over time, and the plan needs to take into account the possibility of these changes. The best financial plans have built-in flexibility, so they can manage the unexpected variations in health, lifestyle, and finances that may occur from time to time in your life.

Your planner will contact you and arrange a time to get together to have a good look at the recommendations. This is an important meeting, and will probably take a couple of hours to complete. It will be a detailed discussion of what the planner was trying to achieve on your behalf, how s/he came to the conclusion that this was the best option, what the outcome is likely to be, any associated risks, and the cost of implementing, maintaining, and reviewing your investments.

Your role in this event is to ask as many questions as you need, to clarify any issues. You are investing a substantial amount of money, and you must be completely sure that this is the right option for you. If it is not, then it will be back to the drawing board, and a revised plan will need to be done to address your concerns. It is rare that this happens, as you are working with a professional who is trained in questioning techniques which will bring out your core values. Changes are usually minor, and do not require a complete revision of the plan.

You will also need to understand the recommendations, and ask for clarification if you are unsure of anything. The presentation of the plan by the planner should give you a clear understanding of the advice, especially if you have taken the time to familiarise yourself with the various aspects of financial planning. The following chapters will do just that.

What Information will be in the Financial Plan? The plan will start by restating your current position, your goals, your risk profile, and your reasons for seeking advice. This provides the basis for the recommendations.

The recommendations have been carefully researched to ensure that they meet your needs. Recommendations will be made in some or all of the following areas:

- Investments
- Tax considerations
- Superannuation and retirement planning
- Retirement income
- Budgeting and cash flow
- Debt management
- Insurance (personal protection)
- Estate planning
- Review process

I have dedicated a chapter of this book to each of the above topics, so that you can be familiar with some of the strategies that may be used to improve your position either immediately or over time.

Your plan will also outline all the costs associated with implementing the advice, as well as any fees or commission that your financial planner will earn.

You may wish to obtain advice from one of your other professional team members (accountant or solicitor), and usually it is easy to have a copy of the plan emailed to them so that they, too, can become familiar with your strategy. Even if you do not require their advice, the statement of advice can be used to determine where all your assets are held (this helps with estate planning), and what strategies affect your tax position, which will help in the preparation of your tax return.

Once you are sure that your strategy is suitable to your needs, you are ready to start implementation of the advice. You and your planner will complete the paperwork together. The bulk of the work happens after this, and is done by your financial planner and his/her staff.

They will keep you informed as to their progress, and you will be advised in writing once money has been invested and your insurance is in force (if recommended in the plan). You will receive updates from your product provider, and if you have agreed to an ongoing review service, your planner will review your situation on a regular basis.

SUMMARY

Your financial plan is an instruction book to get you from where you are now to where you want to be in the future. When you meet with your planner, you will need to ensure that the financial plan meets all your needs. If your goals have changed since you last met with your planner, these changes need to be included in the plan. Your role in the process is to:

- Ensure that you are happy with the recommendations in the plan
- Advise the planner of any changes to your goals or current situation
- Have a good understanding of the recommendations
- Ask for clarification if you are unsure of anything

Next, we shall look at the most common types of investments, many of which will be familiar, and some of which may be completely new. You will probably want to invest in many of them, as they all offer different rewards for investors.

CHAPTER 5

Where Is the Best Place To Invest My Money?

*"Our doubts are traitors, and make us fear the
good we oft might win, by fearing to attempt."*

William Shakespeare

There is no "best place" to invest your money. For most people, it is best to have your money in a number of types (asset classes) of investments. Some people believe that it is best to have all your money in cash, or shares, or property, but this is rarely the best option. Each asset class has advantages and disadvantages, and to get all the benefits, you will need to diversify. Financial planners often talk about *diversification*, and this is because it works.

Diversification works to reduce risk not only between the different asset classes, but also within them. Can you imagine investing your whole fortune into the shares of one company, or one property? This could end in disaster if the company had problems, if the property was untenanted for a period of time, or was filled with termites.

The main asset classes are cash, fixed interest, property, Australian shares, and international shares. In this chapter, we will look at all the above investments, including their various sub classes. We will also look at some alternative investments, including *hedge* funds, infrastructure, and venture capital. We will also discuss managed funds, which can invest in a range of asset classes or just one.

This will give you a good background in what is out there, and may help you to work out your preference. You will also find out the benefits and the pitfalls of each type of investment. We also look at suitable time frames for each investment. You can then discuss this with your financial planner during the risk profiling session, to clarify any points of interest.

Before I discuss the various asset classes, I must first explain what a *managed fund* is. It is impossible to discuss all the types of investments available without mentioning managed funds, and I shall go into detail on types of managed funds later in this chapter.

A managed fund is a professionally managed investment portfolio in which you can buy "units" to represent the amount you have invested. Each managed fund has a specific investment objective and may invest in cash, fixed interest, property, shares, or a mix. The money you invest is used to buy assets in line with this investment objective. The *fund manager* will often be a bank, or owned by a bank. Examples are BT which is owned by Westpac, and Colonial First State, which is owned by the Commonwealth Bank. They can also be owned by one of the major insurance companies, such as AXA, or may not be affiliated with either, such as Aberdeen Asset Management.

When you purchase units in a managed fund, the value of your investment is reflected by the unit price. This can change daily as the value of your investment rises and falls. For example, if you own 100,000 units in a managed fund, and you purchased when the unit price was $1.00, then your original investment was $100,000. If the unit price increases to $1.20, then your investment is now worth $120,000.

CASH

Cash   This is the ultimate short term investment. There is nothing else that works in the short term, and that is why we all need some cash. We all have short term needs and, while we often don't spend too much time thinking about it, this is an important part of your planning. If you are deferring decisions until the stressful (emotional) period has passed, as recommended in this book, then, in that initial period, you will need to have all your money in cash. Once you have met with your financial planner, you will need to set aside cash for not only current expenditure, but also for any major purchases that you may have in mind.

Cash includes a broad range of investments such as "at call" accounts at a bank or other financial institution, cash management trusts, and *short term money market* investments. A cash investment usually has a term of one year or less, meaning that it can be withdrawn within twelve months without penalty. This is generally regarded as the most secure type of investment, as it does not have any rise or fall in capital value.

Cash in this situation is used by the financial institution accepting the deposit. It is used to lend out to clients who wish to borrow money. The price of using the money is known as the interest rate. Like any other business, a bank buys money at a cheaper rate than it sells it. The difference allows them to run their business, and generally make a profit, as well. So, when you deposit money, you will receive less interest than it will cost you to borrow money.

Investing in cash is known as a debt investment. This means that you are effectively investing in someone else's debt. They are paying you (interest) for the use of your money. You have no ownership of their assets, and do not share in the growth or any loss from those assets. Therefore, you should retain your original investment, without loss (or gain) of capital.

The risks you face are based on the borrower's ability to pay you both your interest, and your capital. In Australia, there are regulatory controls on financial institutions, which make it extremely unlikely they could not repay your money. For that reason, this is generally regarded as a safe investment.

Banks and other financial institutions act as a facilitator between you and the borrower, and, of course, provide many other services, as well. They assess credit risks, thereby minimising the chance of loss of interest or capital through bad debts. Because of the pooling of depositors' money, any losses through bad debts will be offset against their profits.

There are many factors that will influence the interest rate. The one that we hear most about is the *Reserve Bank of Australia* (RBA) cash rate. The cash rate is the overnight money market interest rate.

In the early 1990s, the cash rate was 17.5 percent, following the high inflation era of the 1980s. Interest rate increases were used to curb excess demand which had pushed prices up. Inflation has been successfully kept under control since the early 1990s, and so the RBA cash rate has not exceeded 7.5 percent since early 1992.

With the onset of the Global Financial Crisis in 2008, the RBA cash rate fell to a 49-year low of 3 percent in April 2009. This supports the economy by lowering the cost of money, and helps banks to increase the amount of money available for lending. As the economy is now improving, the RBA has started to increase interest rates.

The changing of interest rates to influence economic activity is known as *monetary policy*. Interest rates are changed regularly by the Reserve Bank of Australia (RBA), to control economic activity. Raising interest rates reduces the level of spending and borrowing in the economy and increases the rate of saving, thereby reducing the money supply. Reducing interest rates will have the opposite effect.

The return on your money is also affected by the strength of the financial institution with which you deposit your money. In Australia, we have four major banks: Westpac, Commonwealth Bank, NAB, and ANZ. Because they are the largest and strongest of our banks, they pay less for their money than all other institutions, as they are seen as less risky. They also provide a much larger branch network, and this also comes at a cost. They will, therefore, generally pay you a lower rate of interest.

The type of account in which you place your money will also affect the interest rate. If you have your money in a *transaction account* (this may be a cheque account, or one which you use for most of your transactions), then this will usually give little or no interest. This is because the bank is providing facilities such as branch staff, automatic teller machines (ATMs), statements, internet banking, and telephone banking for generally very low fees. Instead of charging the actual cost for each transaction, they reduce the interest on the money to offset the costs. Accounts which only provide internet facilities, and which charge high transaction costs, will pay higher rates of interest.

As a Windfall Club member, it will often be advisable to have two accounts: a transaction account and an internet-only account. You can keep the bulk of any money you wish to keep in cash in the internet account, and move it across to the transaction account as required. That way, you will be maximising your interest, whilst still having access to a full range of banking facilities.

The greatest risk with a cash investment is that you may get a negative return in real terms. Let me explain. You have just had a great windfall, and have decided that you don't like risk, so will put it all into cash. Sound sensible? Well, maybe not. Let's say with all your money invested in cash, you are now in the top tax bracket, presently 46.5 percent in Australia, including the *Medicare levy*.

You will not pay this rate on all your money, as we have marginal tax rates in Australia, which means that a higher rate of tax is only charged on higher levels of income, not on your total income. So, your average tax may be 40 percent. Your investment is paying you 5 percent, and this is enough for you to live on. Well, the first thing you are going to lose is the tax payable on your investment.

$5\% \times 0.40 = 2\%$ This is how much you will pay in tax.
$5\% - 2\%$ tax $= 3\%$ This is how much you will keep.

Now, the next thing you will lose is purchasing power, due to the effect of increases in the price of goods and services, known as inflation. The RBA uses monetary policy (changes in interest rates) to control inflation, and they have a target of not more than 3 percent increase in inflation per annum. They are usually successful in keeping inflation under control, so we will assume in the example above that inflation is at 3 percent.

3% return after tax − 3% inflation = 0% real return.

So, whilst this may seem a safe investment, it is usually not appropriate for your entire windfall. You are actually getting no return on your money at all in the above example, and if inflation increases, taxes increase, or interest rates fall, then you will have a negative return.

We all need cash for our day-to-day living. It is an essential part of life, and of any investment strategy. It is important to put your windfall into cash in the first instance, when you are not ready to make a decision, and during the preparation phase of choosing a financial planner, accountant, and solicitor.

You will also need to keep it in cash whilst you are obtaining advice from your professional team. Your long term cash requirement will be determined according to your risk profile and your need for cash over the ensuing years.

SUMMARY Cash will return regular income which will increase when interest rates rise, and decrease when interest rates fall. It will also provide capital security (no capital growth or loss) and easy access to your money. Once you have your financial plan, there will be a recommendation to keep some portion of your investment in cash.

FIXED INTEREST

Fixed interest is similar to cash, only the term is usually greater than one year. This gives it different characteristics. You may not be able to get access to it whenever you want, or there may be a penalty if you wish to withdraw prior to the end of the term.

Longer term investments attract a higher rate of return than cash, as you will want to be compensated for lack of access to your money. Typically, the longer you invest, the higher the rate (normal yield curve), although there are exceptions to this. If rates are high but expected to fall in the future, you may get a lower rate of interest on longer terms (inverted yield curve).

The main disadvantages of fixed interest are that it is not usually a part of your portfolio that gives great returns, and if you are spending all the income, then it, too, is eroded by inflation. There are various types of fixed interest funds. I have given a short summary of each below.

Term Deposits These are offered by major financial institutions, and offer a fixed term and a fixed interest rate. They are secure and, therefore, do not offer high levels of interest. They can pay income at a chosen interval, commonly monthly, quarterly, half yearly, or yearly. They are offered for terms of one month to up to five, or sometimes ten, years. As with any fixed interest investment, longer term investments can be disappointing, as the money returned to you has a much lower value than when you invested.

The income from a term deposit must be paid to your nominated bank account. So if you keep your term deposit for, say, five years, then the value of the money invested will be a lot less when you take it out, because of inflation. See below.

> $100,000 invested for 5 years.
> Value at end of term: $100,000
> Real value at end of term, assuming 3% inflation: $85,875

SUMMARY Term deposits provide regular fixed income and no opportunity for capital growth or loss. You may pay a penalty if you redeem them prior to maturity.

Government Bonds *Government bonds* are issued when the government wishes to borrow money for public works, or for any expenditure it may have. As these are secure (Australia has never defaulted on these), they offer a low rate of interest compared to other forms of fixed interest. These are a wholesale investment, and if you wish to invest in these, then you will need to do so using a managed fund.

These investments are for a set period of time, say, five or ten years, and have a set interest rate for the term of the bond, known as a *coupon rate*. This is paid at a regular frequency throughout the term of the bond. For example, you may invest for ten years, with a coupon rate of 7 percent. If you invest $1,000,000, then you will get a return of $70,000 every year for ten years. At expiry, your initial capital will be returned to you in full.

Government bonds are traded daily on the bond market, and this is where the security of the capital may be at risk. Let's look at what happens if interest rates increase. Your managed fund has invested $1,000,000 on your behalf with a coupon rate of 7 percent. The RBA meets, and decides to increase rates to 8 percent. So any new bond investors will receive $80,000 per annum for the next ten years. If your fund wants to sell the bond with the 7 percent coupon rate, then no one will want to pay $1,000,000 for it, as they can now invest at 8 percent. So the bond will be discounted to a level where the effective return for the rest of the term will be 8 percent. For this reason, the longer it is until the end of the term, and the greater the proportional increase in interest rate, the greater the discount that will be applied to its value.

Conversely, if interest rates fall, then your bond will increase in value. The simple way to remember this is that the value of the bond goes in the opposite direction to the interest rate. If rates rise, your investment will fall in value, and if rates fall, then your investment will be worth more. What if your fund does not trade its bonds? They still have to value them at the market price, so you will have volatility (rises and falls) of capital value in any bond fund. The greater the movement in interest rates (as a percentage of the previous rate), the greater the volatility.

For this reason, this is also a medium to long term investment. Interest rates will rise and fall, and if you have suffered a capital loss, this will be returned to you once interest rates have fallen to their previous levels. Of course, if you receive a *capital gain* in the short term and wish to change your investment at that point, then that will work in your favour.

As government bonds are bought using a managed fund, the fund manager will generally allow reinvestment of your income, if this is what you require. This is not a feature of government bonds themselves, and can be arranged by the fund because of the pooling of money. Reinvested money is used to purchase more bonds. This feature also applies to mortgage funds.

SUMMARY Government bonds provide regular fixed income and there is some opportunity for capital growth or loss as interest rates move. At maturity, the initial capital is returned.

Mortgage Funds These are different from government bonds in that, although they fit into the fixed interest sector, the interest rates are not fixed. You can (once again, through a managed fund), lend your money to people wishing to purchase property. The advantage of this over cash is that you are getting the lending rate (less a fee for the fund manager) rather than the deposit rate. As interest rates rise and fall, so will your income. So, if the fund is paying 7 percent per annum when you invest your windfall, then rates increase to 8 percent per annum, your income will increase, instead of being locked into a fixed coupon rate as with a government bond. Conversely, if rates fall, then your income will decrease.

There is a variety of mortgage funds on the market, some offered by large fund managers and banks, and others which can be managed by solicitors and smaller managers. Loans managed by solicitors may be very risky, have a higher rate of default than bank-arranged loans, and often have no diversification, as typically all your money will be lent to one borrower. This type of investment is not one I would ever recommend.

When I was working in country NSW in the early 1990s, these loans were quite common, and some of my clients (prior to meeting me) had invested with various solicitors to increase their income as interest rates were low at the time. A number of these clients later reported that the income had stopped (this was during the "recession that we had to have") and there was no access to the capital, and some doubt as to whether the capital would be repaid. These loans usually offer up to a couple of percentage points' greater return, and can look like a good deal. It is important to realise, though, that if people are paying more for their loans; it is because they are risky borrowers.

When I first started in financial planning and had not had anything to do with these funds, I was talking to an acquaintance who was complaining about the amount of interest he was paying on his loans through a local solicitor. I was employed at a major bank, so suggested that he see one of our lending staff to improve his cash flow by reducing his interest rate. "Oh, the banks wouldn't touch me," he replied. "I'm too risky for them!"

I have always remembered this conversation, and when I had a client, Joe, ask me recently about a mortgage fund which was offering a higher return than other funds (Fincorp), I related that discussion. It was fortunate that I did, as he chose another investment with a lower return and less risk. Fincorp's fund encountered problems a short time afterwards, and their investors lost their money.

This is one of the most important rules of investing; don't take unnecessary risks especially in an asset class that is one of the safer investments in your *portfolio*. If you turn that into a risky investment, then your whole portfolio has become more risky.

SUMMARY   Mortgage funds provide regular, unfixed income which rises and falls with interest rate movements. There is no opportunity for capital gain, and there may be capital losses from loan defaults.

Hybrid Securities   These are called hybrid because they have some of the characteristics of fixed interest and some characteristics of shares. They are generally used when a company wants to raise capital, and they offer an investment with a fixed rate of return, which may be converted to a share at a later date (convertible notes) or which may benefit from franking credits. Other types of hybrids are preference shares, which rank above ordinary shares when a company is wound up, and which have a set return for a period, then may be converted to ordinary shares at a later date. Income securities are another form of fixed interest investment which are listed on the stock exchange and, as such, will be subject to fluctuations in capital value based on the volume of trade.

SUMMARY Hybrid securities provide regular fixed income and opportunity for capital growth or loss as the value of the securities rises and falls with the value of the underlying company. They may convert to shares at a later date, and may offer a partially tax-paid return.

International Fixed Interest   This has all the same characteristics as Australian fixed interest, with a twist: currency. Currency movements work in the same way as interest rate movements, in that they will have the opposite effect on your investment. I have expanded on currency effects in the section on international shares.

Loans to Friends and Family   These can be the most dangerous investments of the lot. They are unlikely to produce good income, and may result in a total loss of the money invested. If this sounds harsh, it is only because reality can be unpleasant. The other great risk with these investments is the breakdown in relationships that can occur as a result. I do not recommend this, unless you can afford to give the money away, and can deal with it emotionally if it goes pear shaped.

Especially for lottery winners, sports people, and entertainers, these can be a nightmare. Many people think you have money to burn, and that you might as well burn it on them. They may have the intention of paying it back, but subconsciously, they are thinking that you have enough, and won't miss the bit that they got! If you lend enough money to friends and family, you can probably kiss your windfall goodbye.

I shall deal with gifting in Chapter 9, but the short answer to this one is get advice first. Do not, under any circumstances, lend or give money to friends or family until you have had advice and know exactly what you need to support yourself. If your adviser says not to do it, then accept that advice, as it will be supported by analysis to show that this will have a detrimental effect on your financial situation.

I have clients, Betty and Bill, who had some money from an inheritance. They wanted to help their granddaughter and her family to get a better house. They came to me for advice. As they had been intelligent with their money for their whole lives, they were well able to look after themselves without needing that money.

I advised them that it was fine to give the money to their granddaughter, as they would never need it themselves. Also, it was gift, so they were not expecting the money back. Because of this, there was no risk to the relationship, which was clearly important to them. So there are times when this is appropriate. The reason I recommend that you proceed with caution (and advice) is that this is a major cause of financial loss and relationship breakdown for windfall recipients.

SUMMARY   Loans to friends and family are a risk to both your money and your relationships. Always obtain advice before you agree to lend or give money to anyone.

PROPERTY

Property   Property has been the favourite of Australians for many years. We all wish to own our home, and love to invest in "bricks and mortar." It is something that we feel comfortable with, and we all feel that we know when we have bought a real bargain. Most of us are living in a house that we own (usually with a mortgage) by the time we are in our mid thirties, and this is more common in Australia than in many other countries in the world. Property has shown good returns for many years, and is a hedge (protection) against inflation.

Where we described cash and fixed interest as debt investments, we describe property as an equity investment. This is because you have some ownership in the asset. Because of this, your investment is subject to rises and falls in value. You may also hear property referred to as a growth asset. Over time, we expect property to increase in value. It may, in the short term, fall in value. For this reason, your financial planner will tell you that this is a long term investment.

One of the great advantages of property is that it can be used as security for a loan. This means that you can borrow money to purchase the property itself. As a general rule, you can borrow up to 80 percent of the property value. This means that if you want to purchase a property for $500,000, you can borrow up to $400,000. You will need to come up with $100,000, plus stamp duty, legal fees and any other costs. First-time home owners will not pay stamp duty on purchases of $500,000 or under. Of course, a loan is subject to the bank's approval, based on your credit history and your ability to repay (serviceability), as well as a satisfactory valuation of the property you wish to purchase.

There are exceptions to this, in that if you are purchasing a property using a "lo doc" loan (where you declare rather than prove your income), then the amount you can borrow is usually 60 percent. If you wish to borrow more than the above percentages, you will need to pay mortgage insurance, which protects the lender if you cannot repay the loan, and they cannot recoup the full loan amount from the sale of the property.

If you already own a property, you can borrow against it (subject to lending criteria) for almost any purpose, and most people use this facility to buy another property. Borrowing to invest is called *gearing*, and this is a broad topic which I shall not discuss in detail here, as it is another book in itself.

There are also high buy and sell costs for property, and this adds to the term of the investment. It will cost you around 7 percent to buy and sell property, and this includes stamp duty on the purchase, as well as legal fees and both building and pest inspections, (around 4 percent total purchase cost) and agent's commission on the sale of the property. The sale cost is usually about 3 percent, and there are legal fees on this transaction, too.

Janne Ashton

I mentioned earlier that property is an inflation hedge. If inflation is on the rise, then usually we see property prices increase. Therefore, unlike cash and fixed interest, property values are not necessarily eroded by inflation. The term inflation hedge means that it protects us from the effects of inflation.

One of the main disadvantages is that property is both time consuming and expensive to sell. Because it cannot be readily sold, it is known as an *illiquid asset*. *Liquid assets* are those which can be easily or partially converted to cash, at their true value. If you wanted to sell a property and get the cash within a period of, say, a week, then you would have to discount your property to arrange this, if it were at all possible.

Another potential problem with property is that we may not always receive an income. The income we receive from property is known as *rent*, and we rely on tenants to pay the rent, If the tenants don't pay, or if the property has no tenants for a period of time, then we will have no income from that property.

Annual rent on residential property is generally around 5 percent of the value of the property. This is easy to assess, as a 5 percent per annum return on a weekly basis is about 1/1000th of the purchase price. Therefore, if you purchase a property for $500,000, you can expect about $500 per week rent for it. If you buy a property for $650,000, you are likely to receive $650 per week rent.

For commercial (offices), retail (shops) or industrial (factories) property, rents are higher as a percentage of the purchase price, and will usually range from 8 to 10 percent per annum. This is because there is a higher risk with these purchases. A house can usually be easily rented; however, if a shop, office or factory is in a place which is no longer desirable, or if the country is in recession, and there are very few businesses looking for premises, then your property may be vacant for some time and have no rental return.

Commercial, retail and industrial property are not for the faint hearted, and probably not for the windfall recipient, unless they are experienced in these types of property purchases. It is very easy to lose money, as the property is valued as a multiple of the rent. If there is no rent, then these properties are extremely difficult to sell.

Residential property is a safer investment, and this can also have its problems, especially in the short term. Many people have lost money on residential property, but rarely if it is held for over five years. The biggest risk is changing your mind shortly after you purchase, as this will nearly always cost you money.

Let's say you get a large windfall, and decide to move house. This is a fairly typical wish of Windfall Club members. If you are going to move to a nicer house in your suburb, then this is likely to work for you. What some people do is move to a suburb which has always been out of their reach financially. This causes problems on a social level, as they may be too far from their friends, they may not get on with their new neighbours, or their friends may feel jealous.

The way to get around this is to rent in the new suburb for, say, six months. This will give you a feel, not only for living there, but also for how it works for you socially. You can then decide whether you still want to live in that area without any major cost. What you have paid to rent in the new suburb may be at least partially offset by rent on your own home.

SUMMARY Property provides income (rent) and the opportunity for capital growth (or loss). This type of investment is only appropriate over the long term (more than five years). Property is a hedge against inflation, is illiquid (not easily converted to cash), and has fairly high buy and sell costs. It is also a favourite of many Australians.

Property Securities Property securities are property trusts that are listed on the stock exchange. The largest of these in Australia is Westfield, which is a major shopping centre provider. As you are purchasing using the Australian Stock Exchange (ASX), then this has characteristics which are unlike those of "real property."

Listed property trusts invest in retail property (shopping centres), commercial (offices), industrial (factories), and sometimes leisure (theme parks). As such, they are paying higher income than residential property, and the income is usually between 7 percent and 9 percent.

Property securities are influenced by both the underlying value of the property, and also the volume of trade on the stock exchange. Therefore, in boom times, the price of the property securities may increase when there has been no change in the underlying value. Conversely, in tough times, you may be able to purchase at a lower price than the actual value of the property. The income from property securities may include some tax-paid or tax-deferred income. This simply means that you will not pay tax on all the income which you receive from this investment.

The volatility of property securities is usually around half the volatility of shares. This means that if the sharemarket rises by 10 percent over a period of time, then the property securities will usually rise by around 5 percent. And, if the sharemarket falls by 10 percent, then property securities will probably fall by 5 percent. For this reason, it is considered a more conservative investment than shares. Currently (2009) we are experiencing more volatility in property securities than in shares, and this is uncommon. You can buy property securities directly, through a broker or online broking house, or through a managed fund.

SUMMARY Property securities are different to real property in that they are listed on the stock exchange, which provides liquidity, and also influences their value. They have higher volatility than real property, as they are valued daily on the stock market. They most often invest in retail, commercial and industrial property. Property securities often provide cheaper entry and exit costs than real property, and may provide tax advantaged income.

SHARES

Australian Shares Australia used to be a country of mainly property owners, and shares were mainly purchased by institutions and the wealthy. This has changed over the last 20 years or so. There have been two factors that brought about this change.

First, the *floats* of some of Australia's major companies, such as Telstra, Commonwealth Bank, AMP, and NRMA (listed as Insurance Australia Group or IAG) brought many people into the sharemarket who would not have previously invested. In the case of AMP and NRMA, shares were issued to members, so without even purchasing shares, they became share owners.

Second, with the advent of compulsory employer superannuation in 1992, nearly all Australia's employees became share investors through their superannuation funds.

Shares are, like property, an equity investment. You will often hear them referred to as equities. When you buy shares, you are purchasing a portion (share) of a company. This entitles you to a share of the profit and an income from the company, which is known as a *dividend*.

Shares can be purchased via an initial public offering (IPO), which is otherwise known as a float. You may also purchase shares through dividend reinvestment, or an offer from the company to buy more shares (rights or bonus issue). The above methods of share purchase are all referred to as buying shares on the primary market. When you buy shares on the primary market, the company is issuing more shares and so effectively selling some of its equity to you. In return, the company gets some money, which it can use for its existing projects, future expansion or to reduce debt.

The other way to buy shares is on the secondary market, and in Australia this is known as the Australian Stock Exchange (ASX). Purchasing shares on the secondary market does not increase the *market capitalisation* (the number of publicly held shares multiplied by the share price), therefore has no direct effect on the company whose shares you have bought. It is just a transfer of ownership from one person (or other legal entity) to another. It often has an indirect effect on the company, as it may affect the reputation of the company, and many of the directors own large parcels of shares, so their net worth is affected as well.

The performance of the sharemarket in general is measured by a number of indices. The most commonly referred to are the All Ordinaries and the ASX 200. The All Ordinaries represents over 95 percent of the value (market capitalisation) of Australia's listed companies, and holds most of the shares on offer. The ASX 200 consists of the 200 largest companies (based on market capitalisation) that are listed on the Australian Stock Exchange (ASX). These can be used as a guide to trading on the market, although it is possible for a company's share price to increase when the market has fallen, and vice versa.

Companies in the top 100 (ASX 100) are generally known as *blue chips*. This refers to their safety as an investment and that they are likely to recover from any downturn, because of their size, stability, and often good management. HIH was a notable blue chip disaster, where the company went into liquidation, and the shares ceased to have any value. Consequently, any money invested was lost. This is one of only a handful of Australian blue chip disasters.

There is another index known as the small ordinaries, which consists of companies inside the ASX 300 (top 300 listed companies) and outside the ASX 100 (top 100). You will hear them also referred to as "small caps" ("caps" being short for capitalisation). These companies are seen as higher risk than blue chips, as they do not have the same track record and are clearly not as large.

You may also hear stocks referred to as *penny dreadfuls*. These stocks can usually be bought for less than ten cents per share, and are often illiquid, as they are not in great demand. Some investors have made huge gains from penny dreadfuls, the most notable being those who invested in Poseidon shares in the late 1960s. This share went from 80 cents to $280 in a matter of a few months, and then fell rapidly.

I don't recommend penny dreadfuls, as most people lose money on them. They are highly risky, and the chance of their businesses going bust is quite high. They are often bought on the basis of a tip, and this would have to be the worst way to buy shares. I have rarely heard of a tip paying off. A friend of mine, Ian, invested a couple of hundred thousand dollars on a tip, and has lost 75 percent of his investment, and is not sure whether the share will recover.

As shares are an equity, or growth investment, they can also be borrowed against. The most common form of lending against shares is called a margin loan. These loans use the shares as security, and you can borrow up to 70 percent against the value of the share. The amount you can borrow depends on the share itself, and its volatility. The stability of the company and the liquidity of the shares also have an effect on how much you can borrow. You cannot get a margin loan using penny dreadfuls as security, and you will get the maximum margin against most blue chip stocks.

The stock exchange provides liquidity for shares by bringing together buyers and sellers. Shares can be traded from 10 a.m. to 4 p.m., Monday to Friday, except on public holidays. Liquidity is one of the main advantages with shares, as you can sell most shares on any day that there is trading on the market, and receive your money three working days later. Some shares may still be illiquid, as there are no ready buyers and sellers for that business. These are the smaller companies. There are always buyers and sellers for Australia's larger companies.

So what happens if there are more buyers than sellers? When this occurs, the price will rise, which will encourage more people to sell and fewer people to buy. If there are more sellers than buyers, then the price will fall. This is why there is volatility in share prices. Shares are effectively being auctioned on the ASX on a daily basis.

This is the main disadvantage of shares, and also the main advantage. Volatility can give big gains in the short term, and big losses. I have a client, Mark, who invested $1,000,000 into shares. A little over three years later, they were worth over $2,100,000. He had borrowed his initial $1,000,000, so he sold the shares, and after repaying the $1,000,000, kept the profit of $1,100,000. This was assessable for capital gains tax, but we managed to reduce this to a minimum using some tax effective strategies.

Janne Ashton

Conversely, as I write this, we are going through a period of falling share prices, and this can be difficult to cope with, especially for those who are used to the fabulous times we have had for the four years preceding this downturn. It is for this reason that you must hold shares long term, as a recovery from a fall in prices such as we have seen in 2008 may take a few years.

SUMMARY   Shares provide tax effective income as well as capital growth or loss. They are a long-term investment with potentially high volatility in the short to medium term. Shares provide investors with liquidity and low entry and exit costs, and can be purchased with a small initial investment..

International Shares   These have, of course, the same characteristics as an Australian share. We refer to them as a separate asset class, partly because of the effect of currency, and also because, in almost all cases, they are purchased through a managed fund, as we don't have easy access to direct international shares.

It is common in all countries around the world for people to invest larger amounts of money in their own local market than in any of the other economies of the world. This is partly as they wish to have ownership in the local businesses, and also because they have access to more information about local companies.

As we enter a period of time where the global economy is much more of a reality than at any time in the past, the interest in international shares has increased. Companies such as Nokia, Microsoft, Boeing, and General Electric (GE) are all household names. They are also businesses which operate in fields that are not represented in Australia. So, if you want to invest in a business that develops software on a world scale, or one that makes mobile phones, then this can't be done if you invest only in Australian equities.

The other advantage of investing overseas is that the size of the businesses is usually much larger than most Australian companies. Whilst size is not necessarily an advantage, it certainly can be, as it is often associated with stability and longevity.

Large businesses often have greater diversification, which also provides them with a buffer against hard times. G.E. started out making household appliances, and now most Australians are also familiar with G.E. Money, which does a large amount of household lending.

Remember that we spoke about interest rate rises causing a fall in value in government bonds. Well, if our currency, the Australian dollar (AUD), rises in value, then international assets fall in value. This applies to any overseas asset. It could be shares, property, or fixed interest. Conversely, if the Aussie dollar falls, then international assets rise in value, other things being equal.

Of course, there are many currencies in the world, but we are most familiar with our currency expressed as a value against the United States dollar (USD). This is a fairly good guide, as overseas share funds usually have a significant portion invested in the U.S.

Some funds offer currency hedging, which takes out the effect of the currency, so you are getting the actual return on the investment without the risk (or potential benefit) of the currency fluctuations. It is important to know whether your fund is hedged or not, as this will help you assess the risk. You may also have an opinion as to whether the currency will rise or fall, and if you feel that it is likely to fall, then you may wish to invest in an unhedged fund. You may also like to have some of each, so that you have a winner regardless of what is happening to the currency.

It is also important to know the experience of the manager with international shares. If the people making the decisions on investments are based in Australia, they may have insufficient expertise in overseas markets to make the best decisions on your behalf. The experience and location of the fund manager is crucial in this asset class.

SUMMARY International shares can provide exposure to industries not represented in Australia, and to companies far bigger than even the largest Australian companies. The value of international shares (and other international assets) is affected by currency movements, thus adding an extra dimension to the investment.

Shares or Property?   Shares and property are both equity investments and, as such, their capital value will grow over the long term, and may fall in value over the short term. It is essential that you have some growth assets in your portfolio, or you will have declining real wealth over time.

The main difference between shares and property is the volatility of prices. Property is valued when it is bought, and sold. As this is commonly many years apart, then we do not regularly see the price of our own property rise or fall. With shares, we see the price move on a daily basis, so we are very aware of the change in value of our portfolio. If you keep your mind on your long term goal, then this can be put into perspective.

Property has a major advantage in that you can live in it, and for the purpose of this discussion, we are comparing investment property, which will not be lived in by the owner. We also like the fact that we can see and feel a property, whereas shares are less tangible. There is also a feeling of being in control, when you can manage the property yourself, but you are unable to control the management of say, BHP.

The advantage of shares over property, other than that returns have historically been higher for shares over most long term time periods, is that you can choose your entry price into shares. Australian real property is, in most areas, expensive, whereas shares can be bought for as little as $1,000. This is also an advantage if you need to sell. If you need some cash for something and have a real property and a share portfolio, then you can sell, say, $5,000 of shares, but you cannot sell the bathroom of your property. We call this divisibility. Shares are divisible, where property is not, unless you are investing in property securities or property managed funds.

You can diversify shares to a greater extent than real property. For example, $100,000 can buy you a property in a country town in Australia, and for the same money, you can buy a portfolio of quality Australian shares. If the country town loses a major industry, then the price of your property may fall and not recover. The reason properties in some country towns in Australia are cheap is because they have had very little capital growth.

As I financial planner, I try to avoid lengthy discussions on "shares or property," as there is room for both in most portfolios. In fact, most people should have both, to have a complete, diversified portfolio. It is like saying, "Which is best, meat, fruit, cheese, or vegetables?" You can cut any of these from your diet and still survive, but for most people, a mix of some or all is best.

If I am pinned down as to which is better, then I have to say that it depends on the circumstances of the individual who is investing. The whole art to financial planning is tailoring the recommendations to suit the client, not in providing a "one size fits all" approach.

MANAGED FUNDS

Managed Funds   These are not an asset class in themselves. They are merely a way of investing into various asset classes. Managed funds are offered by a number of institutions, including specialist fund managers, banks, merchant banks, and sometimes agricultural firms.

Managed funds allow investors to choose a level of investment that they are happy with, subject to a minimum amount (often as low as $1,000), and contribute that much into the managed fund. The managed fund may invest into separate asset classes, or into a mix of many asset classes.

Fund managers employ analysts to research the markets into which they invest. Let's say the fund manager wishes to invest in Australian shares from the ASX 200. Their analysts go through the financials of the top 200 listed stocks, and look to see which of these companies has the best growth or income prospects. They will also look at the markets in which they operate, the management of the company, and their product or service, to get a full picture of how rosy they feel the future will be for that business. On the basis of their research, they will recommend which shares should be in the fund.

This research should allow the managed fund to outperform the market, even after the manager's fees, which are usually around 1 to 1.5 percent of the funds under management.

Another advantage of managed funds is that it allows smaller investors into markets that they would otherwise not be able to enter. In previous sections of this book, I have mentioned that government bonds, and to some extent real property, are often not available to personal investors. Certainly, many people can afford to buy a residential property. Managed funds invest only into non-residential property, and it would be difficult for most investors to purchase an office tower in a major Australian city. By investing through a managed fund, this is well within the reach of most Australians.

They also allow a level of diversification that is often unavailable through direct investments. A typical balanced fund has 30 to 50 Australian stocks, about the same number of international shares, probably about a hundred different commercial, industrial, and retail properties, some government bonds, a number of mortgages, and some cash. Even with a substantial windfall, this diversification would not be obtainable.

In the 1990s, most managed funds were offered by the institution who owned the fund manager. So, if you wanted a managed fund set up by a bank, you would go to the bank and see their adviser, and invest your money. If you wanted to have a range of managed funds, then you went to various fund managers, and bought some units in their funds.

During the 1990s, the system changed, and now most investments into managed funds are done through a master trust, or a wrap account. A master trust is an administration service that allows you to place your money into a variety of managed funds, and sometimes direct shares, using only one account. The master trust or wrap account does all the reporting, so that your statement and tax information for all your investments is consolidated into one report.

SUMMARY Managed funds allow you to invest in a range of investments and/or asset classes within one investment. You are using the services of a team of experts who use research and analysis to provide the basis on which to choose the investments. Managed funds also allow you to choose a level of investment which is comfortable for you.

Diversified Funds These are usually set up to replicate the various risk profiles. For example, if you have done your risk analysis with a financial planner, and you have been assessed as a balanced investor, then your investments should look something like this.

BALANCED FUND—TYPICAL ASSET ALLOCATION

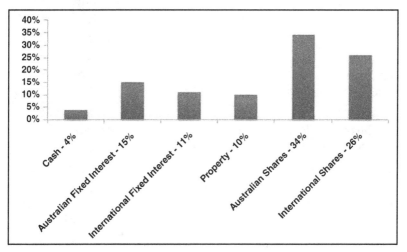

A diversified fund manager will set up the investments in the asset classes pretty much as shown here, and call this a balanced fund. As these are commonly set up by one fund manager, you are getting that manager's Australian share fund, international share fund, and property fund, along with fixed interest and cash.

The problem with this is that whilst they may have a good Australian share fund, the international fund may not be so good. I mention this as that was exactly the case with one of my previous employers. For this reason, I rarely use diversified funds, and prefer to use sector funds, which only invest into one sector, such as property. This problem can be overcome by multi-manager funds, which use different fund managers for different sectors. Diversified funds are very good for small investors, who only have a small amount to invest.

The other disadvantage with these types of funds is that you cannot separate the assets. Say, for example, the market is in a downturn, and you want to draw out some cash. You cannot separate the cash in the fund, so every time you draw some money out, you are selling shares and property, fixed interest, and cash. You may then have to take a loss on your shares and/or property, just because you need some cash.

When you invest through a managed fund, you are getting an expert to look after your money for you. I have at times had complaints from clients who feel that they shouldn't be paying fees to a fund manager when their money has fallen in value.

Although this sounds reasonable, the manager's job is not to get positive performance when the market drops. This is just impossible for a traditional fund. Their job is to pick the better performing stocks, and many of them do this consistently. There are performance figures put out each month for managed funds, and these clearly show who the better performers are.

Whilst this is not particularly comforting if you are paying fees and watching your investment fall in value, it is worthwhile to remember that there are times that growth investments have negative growth, and the returns in the good times will make it all worthwhile. If you want a fund that usually doesn't go down in the tough times, then they are available, too. These types of funds are called absolute return funds, or hedge funds. A fund which is protected from falls in value of the market is called a capital guaranteed or capital protected fund.

SUMMARY A diversified fund is a managed fund which invests into a number of different asset classes within the one fund. These are a good way for small investors to gain exposure to a variety of investments within a range of asset classes.

Hedge Funds   These go in and out of fashion, and there are some consistently good hedge fund managers. The idea of a hedge fund is to produce positive returns at all times. It is, therefore, a "hedge" against falling markets.

Hedge fund managers use a number of strategies. The strategy of a traditional manager is to "buy and hold," until the price of the share rises. One of the most well-known absolute return fund strategies is short selling. This is a strategy for a falling market, where shares are borrowed, then sold. They are then repurchased at a lower price. The shares are then returned, and the profit is kept by the manager.

There are other strategies that are used, as well. Some of the more common ones are arbitrage, which takes advantage of differences in pricing in various markets. For example if an item (it may be a commodity, a currency, an interest rate) is being bought for $2.00 in one market, and $2.50 in another market, then an arbitrage manager will buy at $2.00 and sell at $2.50, and keep the profit.

Another strategy is a merger strategy. When a company is to be taken over, what most often happens is that the company being bought has a rise in its share price, whilst the company that is buying has a fall in its share price. Absolute return fund managers will sell the company that is buying, and wait for the share price to fall, and then buy it back. They will buy the company that is being taken over, wait for the share price to rise, and then sell it. This is a valid strategy, and has its limitations in that if there is no merger activity, then there is not much opportunity to make money.

Hedge fund managers may use some or all of these techniques, and others as well. Another common feature of these funds is that they are frequently offered as a "fund of funds." This means that the manager will combine a number of hedge funds into one fund. This is a way of minimising risk. The manager of the fund will then conduct risk assessment on all the contributing managers. One of the methods of assessing risk is to look at the returns of the funds. If one has a return well above all the others, it may be a sign that the fund is too risky.

Hedge funds have had trouble at times because of high levels of gearing (borrowing). This can magnify gains as well as losses, so in hard times, the falls may be greater than what you would expect in an ungeared fund. It is important to know before you invest in a hedge fund what the levels of gearing are, the track record of the fund manager, and whether it is a fund of funds. This will help you to assess the risk.

The other thing to note with hedge funds is that whilst they will be your favourite funds when markets are falling, they may give lower returns in the good times. A typical hedge fund will average around 7 to 8 percent per annum return. This looks great in the bad years, but when share funds are producing 20 percent return, it looks a bit boring. They are one of the few managed funds that frequently don't pay income, which is another point to consider when assessing whether it is right for you. It all comes down to what you want from your money.

SUMMARY Hedge fund managers use different strategies from traditional fund managers, with the purpose of giving investors positive returns regardless of the performance of the market in which they operate. Their funds are known as hedge funds or absolute return funds.

Capital Guaranteed Funds We are currently experiencing times of high volatility (2009). This is unprecedented in our lifetimes, and is causing discomfort for many people. Fortunately, there are some products which provide a guarantee over your funds (where the amount you invest is protected) and others which provide a rising guarantee, in that they protect both your original investment and the gains on your investment.

Traditionally, capital guarantees were offered over funds which invested only in cash and fixed interest. These gave low returns, and for this reason lost popularity in all but the most volatile times in other markets.

More recently, capital guarantees have been offered over funds which invest in shares, giving investors protection against the volatility which may in the past have put them off investing in share funds. There are a number of ways of providing this protection. One method, known as "bond plus call," invests the bulk of your money into a government bond. A guarantee period is set (say 10 years) and, over the guarantee period, the bond will produce sufficient income to return the value of your original investment. The balance of the money (that was not invested in the bond) will be invested into options over shares, and this provides a return which replicates the return on the underlying shares. In times of low interest rates, either the amount exposed to the market is very small, or the guarantee period is very long. This is because the return on the bond cannot quickly replace the money that has been invested into options. The result for the investor is often poor returns or a guarantee period so long that it is unattractive.

Another common way to provide a capital guarantee is threshold management. This is also known as Constant Proportion Portfolio Insurance (CPPI). A formula is used which allows participation in the market whilst it is rising, and will sell out of the market after a certain percentage fall. This can give poor returns in volatile times, as the investment is sold and invested in cash. When the market rebounds, generally the return is missed, as it is held in cash. As volatile times are when you need the guarantee, then, although your capital is protected, returns are usually poor.

Both of the above methods provide little flexibility for the investor, in that there is a limited range of funds, and little or no option to switch between funds or participate in the guarantee prior to the end of the guarantee period.

A recently released capital guaranteed style of product uses dynamic hedging. This allows investors to choose from a large range of managed funds and charges an "insurance premium" each year for protecting the capital. It is possible to participate in the guarantee prior to the end of the guarantee period, and the product provides flexibility unseen in previous capital guaranteed products.

This is the ultimate way to ensure that you protect yourself, if you are concerned about volatility, and still want access to

Janne Ashton

good returns. It is important to raise this with your financial planner, if capital security is important to you.

SUMMARY Capital Guaranteed investments protect your investment from falls in capital value. Most have some lack of flexibility and involve having a high proportion of your investment in cash for some or all of the investment time frame. Dynamic hedging allows flexibility, with the ability to remain fully invested at all times, and also offers a rising guarantee.

Agribusiness These managed funds invest in agricultural projects, and are usually advertised in the last three months of the *financial year*. The reason is that investment into these funds has been tax deductible, and so they proliferate as the financial year draws to a close, and are attractive to people looking to minimise their tax. The typical products are trees, olives, almonds, and wine.

The reason the government has offered tax deductions is that they would like to encourage investment in these products, and because there is such a long time before any income is received (they have to grow to maturity), it makes it difficult to stimulate interest. Of course, a tax deduction makes them very interesting!

Many of these tax deductions are now not available, as these industries have grown from their infancy. The tax office rulings can change from time to time, and the information as to what is available is made public in March or April each year.

These investments suit high income earners who are looking for long term growth, with no income requirements in the medium term to long term. By long term, it can mean eight years or more. In recent times we have seen the collapse of two of the major agribusiness fund managers: Timbercorp and Great Southern. This has meant that investors have lost their money and potentially the tax deduction that they hoped to achieve. This highlights the fact that any investment needs to be considered in terms of the quality of the investment, and not just its ability to reduce income tax. We live in unusual times, and if we learn anything from the past couple of years it should be the following:

- Diversify your investments
- Insist on quality
- If you want to invest in something which is risky, make it a very small portion of your overall portfolio
- Get advice before you invest

I had a couple of clients who were interested in agribusiness investments. Our research analysts checked out the available products and advised us not to invest with Timbercorp or Great Southern. Our access to quality research meant that our client's investments are in great shape.

SUMMARY Agribusiness investments suit investors with long time frames, no initial need for income and an appetite for risk. They may be tax effective, and this needs to be considered in light of the investment as a whole and its relevance to the needs of the investor.

Infrastructure Funds Infrastructure refers to transportation services such as rail, road, and air services, gas pipelines, and communications services, or anything which is set up to allow movement of goods and services in an economy. These funds sit somewhere between fixed interest and property on the risk return scale. It is a fairly specialised field and, once again, the track record of the fund manager needs to be looked at closely.

There are not a lot of infrastructure funds on the market, and they are unlikely to be recommended as part of your portfolio. They usually pay fairly high levels of income, and do not expect high levels of growth.

SUMMARY Infrastructure funds are specialised funds which invest in companies whose businesses are involved in transportation services. These funds generally pay high income and have low levels of growth, if any.

Venture Capital   These funds have been gaining popularity in recent years whilst the economy was in a boom. They are also known as private equity funds, and involve investing into a new business which has not yet made a profit or may not even have a market for their product, in some cases. They always have the promise of huge returns, and look like a sure winner. Many involve wonderful technology, which would surely be popular.

Of course, the product or service is only part of the picture. There is the distribution and marketing; there are cash flow considerations, and development costs can blow out. These are highly risky investments and not recommended. This is a very easy way to lose some of your windfall. You would also not expect any income from these funds, often for many years.

You may be offered the opportunity to invest into one of these companies by someone you know, especially if they know that you have just had a windfall. Say no. It is just not worth it.

SUMMARY   Venture capital funds provide the opportunity to invest in businesses which have not yet been established, and have no track record. Because of this, there is no guarantee of any income, or the return of your capital.

Many people who lose their windfalls through investing do so because they go into investments that they don't understand, and then pull out of them for the same reason. This chapter is designed to give you an overview of what is out there. Your planner will make recommendations as to what is appropriate, so you will not be faced with making a decision on your own, on this array of investments. What will happen is that you will have a good understanding from the outset as to what you can expect from each type of investment.

SUMMARY

There are a many types of investments and your financial plan will often include a variety of them. The main asset classes are:

- Cash
- Fixed interest

- Real Property
- Property securities/trusts
- Australian shares
- International shares

These all have their own characteristics, and offer diverse rewards to investors. There is no "best investment" and, for most people, a mix of some or all of the above is best.

There is a range of managed funds offering distinctive investment styles and some alternative investment types. These can give you access to investment choices not otherwise available. Capital protection is a great option if you want the extra return on, say, shares, without the worry of volatility.

Whenever you have lots of money, there is always tax to pay. Of course, with careful planning, you can minimise your tax, and thereby increase the amount you get to keep for yourself. The next chapter goes through how the various windfalls will be affected by tax. But don't worry; I also have information on how keep tax to a minimum.

CHAPTER 6

How Much Tax Will I Pay?

The hardest thing in the world to understand
is the income tax.

Albert Einstein (attributed)

There is a huge variety of taxes in Australia. In this chapter, I shall concentrate on the two which are most relevant to Windfall Club members. As with the rest of this book, the aim is to educate, not to advise you.

You will definitely need tax advice, and this must come from a professional who is qualified to provide it. What you will learn in this chapter are some effective strategies for legally minimising tax. Your professional team (financial planner, accountant, and solicitor) will work with you to find the best solution for your situation.

Your two most important tax questions will be "How much tax will I pay on the lump sum I receive?" and "How much tax will I pay on the income that the windfall generates?" We will look at the answers to both of these questions, and the best ways to legally minimise tax on each. This is extremely important, as the more you pay in tax the less you receive yourself. Whilst I am a firm believer in the role of tax in our society, I am also of the opinion that you have a right to pay no more than what is legally required.

Tax is levied as a way of redistributing wealth and to provide funds for public works. The government (public sector) takes the responsibility for arranging the large projects necessary for a healthy economy. Many of these works are not profitable, and need to be provided regardless of profitability.

The most common publicly funded works are transport infrastructure (roads, railways and airports), healthcare (hospitals and community health centres), utilities (water, sewerage, electricity and gas), communications (telephone and some television stations [ABC, SBS]), education (schools, universities, and TAFE), and public housing. Of course, this is not an exhaustive list of government spending. It does, however, justify the fact that tax is collected, much as we all find it painful at payment time.

Social security is another area that is looked after by the public sector. This is the "Robin Hood" department, in that taxes are taken from those who can afford to pay (the rich), and given to those who cannot financially support themselves (the poor). Of course, we all know that those who pay tax are not necessarily rich, and those who receive social security payments are not necessarily poor, but the concept is still the same.

There are many people who both pay tax and receive social security payments, and these are generally families who are receiving support to ensure that their children are able to live well, or partially self funded retirees who receive a part pension and some income from investments.

The government may also provide services which complement private sector services. As an example, there are many private hospitals in Australia that are operating profitably. So why do we need public (government run) hospitals? Private hospitals need to have paying patients and, for this reason, to get into a private hospital, you generally need to have private health cover. If you are a Medicare-only patient, you can go to a private hospital if you are prepared to pay the cost yourself.

For many people, the cost of hospitalisation, or even private health cover, is out of the question. So it is, therefore, up to the government to ensure that these people have access to quality health care.

Income Tax   This tax affects most adult Australians. We usually get to know it in our first job, often whilst we are at school. We get our first pay, and there is less than what we have actually earned, as some has been paid to the tax office, by our employer.

Janne Ashton

This method of paying tax is known as *"Pay as you go,"* or PAYG.

It is a requirement of the Australian Tax Office (ATO) that employers deduct tax from the salary/wage of their employees and remit it to the tax office on a regular basis. This ensures that tax is paid in a timely manner, and reduces the administration burden for the ATO, as it is only receiving tax payments from each employer, rather than each employee.

Australia uses marginal tax rates. These are shown in the following table.

Tax rates 2009-2010

Taxable income	Tax on this income
$1 – $6,000	Nil
$6,001 – $35,000	15c for each $1 over $6,000
$35,001 – $80,000	$4,350 plus 30c for each $1 over $35,000
$80,001 – $180,000	$17,850 plus 38c for each $1 over $80,000
$180,001 and over	$55,850 plus 45c for each $1 over $180,000

Source: www.ato.gov.au

A marginal rate guarantees that you are never worse off by earning more money. A marginal rate means that you only pay the higher tax on each dollar earned that falls within the new (higher) tax bracket. As an example, let's say you earn $6,000 a year in your part time job. You will pay no tax at all (this is different if you are a school student or a non-resident, but in the main, that is the case).

Your employer asks you to increase your hours, and your pay increases to $7,000 per year. Your tax calculation will be as follows:

First $6,000 – nil tax
Next $1,000 taxed at 15c per dollar. $1,000 × 15c = $150
Total tax: $150.
Net pay: $6,850.

I have often heard people say, "If I earn more money, I end up worse off, as I go into a higher tax bracket." This is simply not true. It would be if rates were not marginal and, using the previous example, this would be the result of your extra work:

$7,000 × 15c = $1,050 tax
Net pay: $5,950.

In this case, you would be worse off by doing extra work. Clearly, this tax system would not provide any incentive to earn more income, hence marginal rates.

As you earn more income, your average tax rate will increase. You can calculate your average tax rate by dividing your income by the total amount of tax you pay. If you work this out as a percentage, then this is the average percent of each dollar that you pay in tax. In the example below, we look at the average tax rate for a person with an income of $75,000 per annum with a marginal rate of 30 cents in the dollar, and the change in the average tax rate if their income increases to $85,000 with a marginal rate of 38 cents in the dollar.

Tax on $75,000 is

| $35,001 – $80,000 | $4,350 plus 30c for each $1 over $35,000 |

($40,000 × 0.30) + $4,350 = $16,350
$16,350 / $75,000 = 21.8%

Tax on $85,000 is

| $80,001 – $180,000 | $17,850 plus 38c for each $1 over $80,000 |

($5,000 × 0.38) + $17,850 = $19,750
$19,750 / $85,000 = 23.24%

This is usually a better measure of how much tax you will pay, as average tax rates don't change much with small increases in pay. When you have a windfall, however, you are likely to have a large increase in your income, and so tax planning is imperative.

Personal Tax   When you earn money in your own name, you pay tax personally. This means you complete an individual tax return and are taxed at the rates shown above. For married couples in receipt of a windfall, the money may be invested jointly so that future earnings are split over two marginal tax rates, thereby lowering the total amount of tax payable. This is known as income splitting. For example, if you have a windfall that gives you an income of $80,000, the tax you will pay will be $17,850, plus Medicare levy (see section below). Let's see how much tax you will pay if you split the money between two people.

$80,000 / 2 = $40,000
Tax on $40,000: $4,350 (tax on $35,000)
      plus $5,000 × 30c.
$5,000 × 30c = $1,500
Total tax on $40,000: $4,350 + $1,500 = $5,850
Total tax on $80,000: $5,850 × 2 = $11,700

So, you have decreased your tax bill from $17,850 to $11,700 just by splitting the money with your spouse. Important for lottery winners, if you are married when you win, your windfall is an asset of the marriage, so you might as well split it anyway! Income splitting is probably the simplest form of tax planning, and one of the most effective.

It becomes a little more complicated if you are both working, and on dissimilar incomes. You may want to adjust the windfall income so that you equalise the incomes between the two of you. This is especially relevant if there is a large disparity of income. If one partner is earning $150,000, and the other is earning $22,000, then splitting the windfall income 50/50 is not necessarily the best option. Of course, your accountant will guide you on these matters so you won't have to work it out for yourself.

You may have the ability to reduce the tax paid on your income, and this is when you have tax deductible expenses. They may be expenses incurred in earning your income, such as income protection insurance, the cost of purchasing tools required to carry out your work, or education expenses relevant to your occupation.

You may also have investments which have deductible expenses, such as rates, insurance and repairs on an investment property, and interest on loans which were used to purchase your investment.

Some investments may be tax deductible (see Chapter 5), and contributions to superannuation may also be tax deductible (see Chapter 7). Contributions to most registered charities also attract a deduction.

Income Tax Provisions for Sports People and Entertainers As their income may be distributed unevenly between the tax years, there are provisions which protect entertainers and sports people from being taxed too highly. These provisions include a number of other professions such as authors, artists, composers, performers, and production assistants.

The tax provisions for people in this category of windfall recipients are quite complex and certainly require the guidance of a professional who specialises in this area. There is a formula to calculate taxable professional income, which apportions deductions between the taxable professional income and other assessable income of the taxpayer. There are also averaging provisions, which spread the tax on taxable professional income.

Calculating Average Taxable Professional Income If a taxpayer became entitled to the averaging provisions less than five years ago, and was a resident for part of the income year immediately before professional year one, the tax on taxable professional income (TPI) is nil in year 1. In year two, one third of the TPI in year 1 is taxed. In year three, ¼ of the TPI in years one and two is taxed and in year four ¼ of the income in years 1, 2 and 3 is taxed. This is a double-edged sword, as although you pay less tax initially, you may still be paying tax after your professional income has ceased.

A taxpayer's professional Year 1 is the first income year:

- During which the taxpayer was an Australian resident (for all or part of the income year); and
- For which the taxpayer's taxable professional income was more than $2,500.

A taxpayer can have only one professional year 1.

Medicare Levy   Medicare is the government-administered system used in Australia to provide medical care for all Australians. Whenever you require medical care, you will be asked to produce your Medicare card.

Medicare subsidises visits to hospitals and doctors, and this is funded by a levy which is paid by any Australian resident who is paying income tax. The levy is placed on each dollar of taxable income, and is normally 1.5 percent.

For example, if your taxable income is $50,000, then you will pay, on top of your income tax, $750 in Medicare levy.

$$\$50,000 \times 1.5\% = \$750.$$

There are exemptions from the Medicare levy for low income earners (this shouldn't be relevant if you have just had a windfall) and there is a surcharge (1 percent) for high income earners if you do not have private health cover. The Medicare surcharge may now be relevant, as it may not have been an issue for you in pre windfall times, but as a result of higher income may well be now. For singles, you will pay the surcharge if your income is over $73,000. For couples, the threshold is $146,000. The threshold increases if you have more than one child.

Companies   Investing using a company is different from owning investments yourself, in that the company is a separate legal entity. You are a shareholder of the company, and if you take money from the company, you will pay tax on it, unless the company is repaying a loan from you. If you invest your money through a company, the company will pay tax at a different rate than you will as an individual. In Australia, companies pay tax at a rate of 30c in the dollar. Unlike personal tax, there are no marginal rates, just a flat rate of tax on every dollar earned (after expenses). There is also no Medicare levy for companies, as a company does not require medical attention.

You will notice that the company tax rate is much lower than the top marginal tax rate. This may be relevant to you, in that there are times when it is appropriate to invest your money using a company structure.

For example, if you are on the top marginal tax rate and you invest through a company, you will reduce by 15 cents in the dollar, (plus Medicare levy) the amount of tax paid on any income received over $180,000. The trap is that if you want to use the money yourself, you will have to pay the extra 15 cents in the dollar to access it anyway. There may be times when this is an appropriate structure to use, but for most people this will not be the case.

I mention this because I often see clients with unnecessarily complicated tax structures that appear to serve no useful purpose. Capital gains tax is higher for companies than individuals, and most people under the age of 55 are investing more for growth than income. Those 55 and over can use superannuation as a far more effective strategy. More about that later.

Family Trusts   There is a variety of trusts available that have been touted as the great tax saviour, however, most of the loopholes that made them attractive have been closed. A trust is simply where an asset is held on behalf of someone else, therefore, in trust.

A family trust allows you to distribute income to various family members (who are considered to be beneficiaries of the trust). The level of distributions can be changed from year to year, according to the financial circumstances of the family members. This is called a discretionary trust, as you have discretion as to who receives the income.

For example, a child can only receive $2,667 unearned (investment) income per year, tax free. So, when your child turns 18 and can receive investment income as an adult, the distribution to that child may increase.

The trust must distribute all its income in the financial year in which it is earned, or it will be taxed at the top marginal rate. If it needs to be distributed after the end of the financial year, this is all right, as long as it is counted by the recipient as being earned in the year it was received by the trust.

For most people, both trusts and companies are unnecessary complications, and they involve extra expense both in setting up, and in ongoing management and accounting. There are situations where they are both appropriate and effective, and your professional team will advise you as to whether they will work for you.

Superannuation   This is a whole chapter on its own, as this is an investment with tax advantages like no other. Please go to Chapters 7 and 8 for a full explanation of all the goodies that superannuation can offer.

Dividend Imputation   When a company declares a dividend, it will distribute the dividend in one of three ways. The dividend can be fully tax paid, and this is called fully franked. The company may have paid no tax, and this is an unfranked dividend. If some of the tax has been paid, then the dividend is partially franked. Any tax that has been paid is often referred to as an imputation credit, and this will show on your dividend statement.

If a company has paid a fully franked dividend, then it has paid tax at the company tax rate of 30 cents in the dollar. If your tax rate is 30 cents, then you will pay no income tax on the dividend. If it is less than 30 cents, then you will get a refund, and if it is over 30 cents, then you will pay the balance, that is, the difference between your tax rate and 30 cents in the dollar. On an unfranked dividend, you will pay full tax, and on a partially franked dividend, you will pay full tax on the unfranked portion, and the franked amount will be treated as explained above.

Whilst this is not a tax benefit, as you will not pay any more or less tax than any other investment, you will need to "gross up" any franked dividend by 30 percent to get the true rate of return. For example, let's assume you receive a fully franked dividend of 7 percent. You would like to compare this to another investment which pays 8.5 percent, which is fully taxable. This is how we work out the grossed up value.

Net return / (1 − tax rate)

In this case, the tax rate is 30% (or 0.3), so the formula looks like this:

7/ (1 − 0.3), or put simply, 7/0.7.
This of course, equals 10. (7 is 30% less than 10)

So, although the other investment pays a nominally greater return of 8.5%, the franked dividend pays a higher actual return of 10 percent.

Capital Gains Tax   As we define capital as the principal sum invested (and any further additions to that principal sum), then capital gains tax is levied, not on the capital, but on the increase in value of the principal sum, brought about by an increase in price. For example, if you buy a property for $500,000, spend $100,000 in capital improvements to the house, then sell it for $600,000, you will not pay capital gains tax. The increase in the value of the property has been brought about by your expenditure, not by re-pricing of the asset.

If, however, you had spent an extra $20,000, and then sold it for $600,000, you would have a capital gain of $80,000, which may then be taxed. This is a simple example which does not allow for any buy and sell costs.

Capital gains tax may be assessable on anything which has appreciated in value. If you own an asset for less than one year and make a capital gain, then the full gain will be added to your income and then taxed as income. If you hold the asset for one year or more, you will only pay tax on 50% of the gain. It is, therefore, important (if looking to minimise tax) to hold assets on which a capital gain has been made for a year or longer.

The most common assets that fall into this category are shares and property. You could pay capital gains tax on antiques, paintings and other works of art, and even wine, but for most people, this is not an issue.

To work out capital gains tax accurately, you will need to know the following information:

- Purchase price of the asset
- Cost of any improvements
- Buy and sell costs
- Date of purchase

If the asset was purchased before 20 September, 1985, it is generally not subject to capital gains tax, as this is the date that CGT was introduced in Australia. If the asset was purchased after 19th September, 1985, you add the remaining items in the list above and subtract them from the sale price of the asset, then you have the assessable capital gain. To work out capital gains tax, you need to then discount that figure by 50 percent (halve it) and add the remaining 50 percent on to your assessable income. Remember that this discount is only available for assets held for twelve months or longer.

Let's say Fran earns an income of $50,000 per annum. She has recently sold an investment property in a small country town, which she purchased for $100,000 five years ago. She has just sold it for $180,000. Her expenses were as follows:

- Buy and sell costs: $10,000. This includes stamp duty, legal fees when both buying and selling, and agent's commission on the sale of the property.
- Improvements: $10,000. Fran put in a new kitchen and new carpets.

Her accountant has calculated her capital gain as shown below:

$180,000 (sale price) − $100,000 (purchase price) = $80,000
$80,000 − $20,000 (costs as shown above) = $60,000
$60,000 / 2 = $30,000 (50% discount)

She then adds the $30,000 to her taxable income of $50,000, which gives her a total taxable income of $80,000. Because the $30,000 is all taxed at 30 percent, then her capital gains tax is $9,000 ($30,000 × 30% = $9,000). Her rate of tax on the $60,000 total gain is 15 percent or half her marginal rate, as the tax is only paid on half the gain.

Tax Treatment of Windfall Lump Sums   One of the most important questions to ask when you receive a windfall is, "How much tax will I pay on the money I receive?" The following section will give you information on just that. Taxes take various forms, and we look at all the taxes that are likely to affect you as a windfall recipient.

Some windfalls attract no tax, whilst others are taxed. Some are taxed sometimes and not others. For that reason, I shall deal with the tax treatment of each windfall separately. I have already discussed tax treatment of income for sportspeople and entertainers in a previous section.

Inheritance   There are no death duties in Australia and the assets pass from the *estate* to the beneficiaries without tax being paid. Of course, there are some tricks to estate planning, and these are discussed in detail in Chapter 13.

Assets pass from the estate to the beneficiaries without tax being paid. There may be tax to pay if your inheritance has come from the deceased's superannuation, (this is not capital gains tax, and will be discussed in detail in Chapter 13).

If the asset was subject to capital gains tax in the hands of the deceased, there may be tax to pay. For example, Uncle Harry had a property which he bought for $100,000 ten years ago and

Janne Ashton

it has been used as an investment property ever since. If it is now worth $350,000, the beneficiary may receive the money from the sale of the property, less capital gains tax paid by the estate. If the property is not sold, the beneficiary will receive the property and the tax will not be paid by beneficiary until the property is sold. It is important to get advice in this situation, as a solicitor or estate planning specialist can help you with your tax planning.

Redundancy   I have already mentioned that there are tax concessions for bona fide redundancy. There are four necessary components within this basic genuine redundancy requirement:

- The **payment** being tested must be **received** *in consequence of* **a termination.**
- That termination must involve an employee being **dismissed from employment.**
- That dismissal must be **caused by** the **redundancy** of the employee's position.
- The redundancy payment must be made **genuinely** because of a redundancy.
Source: **www.ato.gov.au**

Payments to employees for bona fide redundancy have a portion of the money which is tax free to the recipient. Below is the bona fide redundancy tax free threshold for the 2009–2010 financial year.

$7,732 + $3,867 for each completed year of service

As an example, we will look at Stefan, who has been with his employer for just over ten years. He has just been made redundant, and has been advised that his employer will pay $50,000 as a redundancy payment. He would like advice on how much of this he can expect to receive tax free. We used the following calculation.

$7,732 + (completed years of service × $3,867)
$7,732 + (10 × 3,867) = $46,402 tax free portion.

The balance will be added to his taxable income. There are transitional arrangements until 30 June, 2012, which allow rollover of the taxable portion to superannuation, for those who have been in a contract of employment prior to 9 May, 2006. This may result in a reduction in tax payable.

Total and Permanent Disability Insurance and Compensation Claims

These may be treated in various ways by the tax office, depending on how they are paid. If you receive the payout as a lump sum from an *ordinary* (not superannuation) life insurance policy, then the proceeds will be tax free. Sometimes, the benefit is paid over a series of payments. This is possible if the life office deems it appropriate because the level of disability may change, as in some motor-neurone disorders, or a stroke. This is known as a structured settlement and will be treated as tax free if it meets certain conditions. It is important that you receive tax advice before accepting a structured settlement, to ensure that you are able to meet the conditions for a tax free payment.

There may also be tax to pay if the payment comes from insurance inside superannuation. Please refer to Chapter 13 for details.

Divorce   Lump sum divorce payments are tax free, as are maintenance payments, as these come from after tax money.

Life Insurance Payout   Generally, the proceeds of a life insurance policy are tax free. When I use the term life insurance, I am referring to all lump sum claims paid out by a life insurance company. These include life insurance, total and permanent disability insurance (TPD), and trauma claims. I have included life insurance in this section, as there is a provision for those with a terminal illness to receive their claim once they are diagnosed as terminally ill.

Some years ago, my client, Albert, had life insurance paid for him by his employer. Shortly after taking out the policy, he was diagnosed with inoperable bowel cancer. I managed to have his claim paid to him before he died, so that he could pay his mortgage, arrange and pay for his funeral, and give his wife $30,000 which she could use for whatever she needed. She also did not have to go through the rigmarole of a claim whilst grieving for her husband.

This payment was tax free. If you are receiving a life insurance payout under a terminal illness benefit, then you can expect that the payment will be tax free, regardless of whether the insurance is held inside or outside superannuation.

This presents a planning opportunity. If you would like your superannuation life insurance to go to your adult children, then normally they will pay tax on the proceeds (see Chapter 13). If you have the opportunity to take it out as a terminal illness benefit, then, because you get the payment tax free, you can give them the money without any tax being paid as there is no gift tax in Australia.

Trauma Insurance   This is a tax free lump sum payment.

Sale of Business   There are extra concessions for capital gains tax for the sale of a small business. This is a highly technical area, and it is important to obtain professional advice, as the points below only cover the basics, and are not a complete analysis of the legislation.

In order to qualify for small business concessions when selling your business, you must satisfy the following basic criteria:

- Must be selling an active asset, that is, it must have been used for carrying on a business.
- Annual turnover of less than $2,000,000, or
- Net assets of client (and affiliated entities) are less than $6,000,000

If you have owned the business for less than 15 years, the normal 50 percent discount for CGT applies, and there is another 50 percent discount that applies as well (this is one of the small business concessions). Let's say you sell a business for $3,000,000, and you have spent $1,000,000 in capital expenses including buy and sell costs. You therefore have a capital gain of $2,000,000. With the two 50 percent discounts applied, your assessable capital gain goes down to $500,000.

$2,000,000 / 2 = $1,000,000
$1,000,000 / 2 = $500,000.

There is also the opportunity to contribute up to $500,000 into superannuation to offset capital gains tax (CGT Retirement Exemption). This is treated as a non-concessional (undeducted) contribution, so is part of the tax-free portion of your superannuation. I shall explain this fully in Chapter 7, but, needless to say, it is an advantage for you. In the above example, you only need to contribute $500,000 to super to bring the tax down to zero. It is important to note that if you have two eligible business owners, they each can contribute up to $500,000 to superannuation.

Let's look at my clients, Mark and Julia, who are looking to sell their jointly owned business (owned less than fifteen years) and have a capital gain of $4,000,000. We can apply the 50 percent discount twice, and that brings their capital gain down to $1,000,000.

$4,000,000 / 2 = $2,000,000
$2,000,000 / 2 = $1,000,000

They can each contribute $500,000 to superannuation. Their capital gain will reduce to zero and, of course, so will their capital gains tax.

There is another concession that can be used by small business to legally avoid capital gains tax. If you have been carrying on a business for fifteen years or more, then you do not pay any capital gains tax. In a situation where you are not paying capital gains tax on the sale of a business, e.g. using the fifteen-year exemption or if the business was a pre CGT asset, you can contribute up to $1,100,000 (indexed annually) from the proceeds of the sale to superannuation.

Because of the intricacies of this legislation, it is important that you obtain advice before you sell your business. It is equally important to obtain advice when starting a business and, at least annually, to avoid problems once you decide to sell. There may be methods of structuring the sale of the business which are much more tax effective, and once the contract for the sale of the business is signed, it may be too late to change. A poorly structured deal may cost you hundreds of thousands of dollars in tax, which may be completely avoided with the right advice.

Lottery Win   In Australia, lottery wins are not taxed. They are not a capital gain, and are instead treated as a prize, which is not taxable. Income derived from the proceeds of the lottery win is usually assessable for income tax (see Chapter 8 for information on tax free income), but there is no CGT on the windfall itself.

SUMMARY

Tax is generally your biggest budget expense. As a windfall recipient, you may pay tax on the income from your windfall, and may pay tax on the windfall itself. The amount of tax you pay varies according to your income and whether you pay tax as:

- An individual
- A partnership
- A company
- A trust
- Superannuation

For individuals, capital gains tax is only levied on half the gain (if the asset is held for twelve months or longer), and tax planning can be used to reduce the amount of both income and capital gains tax that has to be paid.

Now that we have looked at how tax affects each type of windfall, it is now time to see how we can reduce the amount of tax we pay. Superannuation is a "legal tax dodge," and is the government-supported method of retirement saving. In the following chapter, you will see that "super" is not just for the oldies, as it can work for you at any age.

CHAPTER 7

Superannuation: A Legal Method of Reducing Tax

A windfall makes such a sudden change to your life, and you can often feel so wealthy that the details of investing seem unimportant. One of the most important rules of investing is to consider how much tax you will pay, as this affects the overall return on your money. It is, therefore, important to maximise after tax returns. In this chapter, we look at the various ways that superannuation allows you to legally minimise tax at any age. A windfall recipient who ignores superannuation is probably not doing the best with their money.

Superannuation is a complex matter and professional advice is a must. The purpose of this chapter is not to give you all the complexities of superannuation—that would be a whole book in itself. I have given you a simple overview of the most common ways of using superannuation to make the best use of your windfall.

Superannuation (commonly referred to as super) is unlike other investments in that it has the following three features: you will generally pay less tax on superannuation investments than on investments outside super; you may be able to claim a tax deduction on the contributions to super; and there are restrictions on when you can take the money out. The tax saving aspects of superannuation can provide advantages for windfall recipients, as I shall discuss in this chapter.

Superannuation is the preferred method of retirement saving in Australia. The governments of Australia have been supporting superannuation for a number of years, as they all have the same goal, and that is to minimise the number of Australians receiving the age pension. After World War II (1939 to 1945), there was a massive increase in the number of babies born in Australia, and this continued until 1964. This was known as the baby boom, and people born in the years 1946 to 1964 are known as the *baby boomers*.

These baby boomers are now approaching retirement, and this has been a concern for the governments of Australia for a long time, as it has resulted in an aging population. The average age of the country's population is increasing because there is a disproportionate number of people over the age of forty-five. If all these people were to go on an age pension, there would be a massive rise in the tax paid by working Australians, as this would be necessary to fund the age pension payments.

No political party is going to win an election by increasing tax, or by reducing age pension payments. So, for a number of years now, Australian governments have been trying to improve superannuation so that it is attractive enough for people to save for retirement and, at the same time, attractive enough to keep funds invested in super once retired, rather than spend it all and then claim the age pension.

This has resulted in regular changes to superannuation, which tends to make it seem complex and difficult. Certainly, the changes have made it an area in which professional advice is essential, and this book is not designed to be used to replace that advice. The information given below about superannuation is to give you an outline of what can be achieved using superannuation, and some of the great benefits available to you.

CONTRIBUTIONS TO SUPERANNUATION

Of course, with all the tax benefits of superannuation, there have to be some restrictions. Otherwise, everyone would put all their money into it, and the government would suffer a severe loss of tax revenue.

Who Can Contribute to Superannuation?   If you are between the ages of 18 and 65, then generally you are eligible to contribute to superannuation. After age 65, it gets trickier, and you have to pass a "work test." The work test demands that you work at least 40 hours within a 30-day period, at least once within the financial year that you contribute. This can often be arranged if you have self-employed friends or family, who are happy to give you some work to satisfy this work test. Having more money in super in retirement is such a bonus in retirement that it is worth trying to arrange work, as any income drawn from superannuation after age 60 will be tax free. As an added bonus, once you are drawing an income (pension phase), any investment return inside the fund will be tax free as well. More about that later.

How Much Can I Contribute to Superannuation?   Until recently, restrictions were put on the amount of money you could withdraw from superannuation on retirement. This was done in the form of tax penalties, so that if you took out more than what was considered reasonable (known as the reasonable benefits limit, or RBL,) then the top rate of income tax was paid on any withdrawal over that limit. Changes came into effect on 1st July, 2007, and now no tax is payable on withdrawal from superannuation after age 60. The catch is that there are now restrictions on how much you can put into super. The maximum contributions to superannuation are as follows:

- $25,000 per year (concessional contributions)—this threshold is indexed each year in line with Average Weekly Ordinary Time Earnings (AWOTE), and rounded down to the nearest $5,000. As this limit commences in the 2009/10 financial year, indexing will commence in the 2010/2011 financial year. A transitional limit of $50,000 per year (until 2011–2012 financial year) applies if you are 50 or over at the end of the financial year in which you contribute (this is not indexed)
- $150,000 per year (non-concessional contributions) or up to $450,000 if the non-concessional cap is averaged over three years (see details below)

- CGT Cap $1,100,000 (indexed each year in line with Average Weekly Ordinary Time Earnings (AWOTE), and rounded down to the nearest $5,000) lifetime limit for eligible business owners (see section on sale of business). This only applies if a business is owned for 15 years or more, and the maximum is $500,000 for CGT rollover.
- Up to $450,000 (non-concessional contributions) can be made in one year, by bringing forward the next two years' contributions; so, instead of contributing $150,000 each year for three years, you can do it all at once, and skip the next two years. You can only do this if you are under age 65 on the first day of the financial year in which the contribution is made. So therefore, the financial year in which you turn 65 is your last opportunity to bring forward up to three years' non-concessional contributions.

The figures above all relate to the maximum amount you can contribute in any financial year (1 July to 30th June). This means that if you get a windfall in, say, June of any year, then you can contribute the maximum amount in June, and then again in July, as you would have entered another financial year in July.

TYPES OF CONTRIBUTIONS TO SUPERANNUATION

Concessional Contributions   These are very important for windfall recipients who have not yet reached retirement age. This is the way to pay less tax on your income, whilst at the same time setting aside money which will provide a tax free income from age 60. Concessional contributions are those on which a tax deduction has been claimed. As all industries love their jargon, these were previously known as *deductible contributions*. These contributions are taxable to the superannuation fund at a rate of 15 cents in the dollar, so it is important to check that your personal tax rate exceeds 15 percent to ensure that you have a real benefit. To find out how much tax you will save, you need to know how much tax you would have paid, so below are the current tax rates for residents. These also appear in Chapter 6.

Tax rates 2009–2010

Taxable income	Tax on this income
$1 – $6,000	Nil
$6,001 – $35,000	15c for each $1 over $6,000
$35,001 – $80,000	$4,350 plus 30c for each $1 over $35,000
$80,001 – $180,000	$17,850 plus 38c for each $1 over $80,000
$180,001 and over	$55,850 plus 45c for each $1 over $180,000

Source: www.ato.gov.au

Let's say you have an income of $80,000, and you wish to contribute $45,000 to super. If you can claim a tax deduction on your superannuation contributions, then you will only pay income tax on $35,000.

$80,000 − $45,000 = $35,000.

As you would have paid tax at 30 cents on each dollar, then this will reduce the income tax that you need to pay by $13,500—a massive saving.

$45,000 × $0.30 = $13,500

So, therefore, people like to make tax deductible contributions to super, particularly those on high incomes. The amount you save is based on the amount that you would have paid in tax if you hadn't claimed a deduction. As a result, the higher your tax bracket, the more you will save by contributing to super. For example, if you contributed the same $45,000 to superannuation, and your income was $150,000, then you would save $17,100!

$45,000 × $0.38 = $17,100 reduction in income tax

As I mentioned earlier, whilst you have a massive income tax saving, you are paying tax within your superannuation fund at a rate of 15 percent. So on a concessional contribution of

Janne Ashton

$45,000, your superannuation fund will pay $6,750 to the ATO. As this rate is lower than the marginal rates in the examples above, you are still much better off after having made concessional contributions to superannuation if your marginal tax rate is 30 percent or higher.

Superannuation Guarantee Contributions (SGC) In 1992 it became compulsory for employers to make superannuation contributions on behalf of their employees. For this reason it is also known as compulsory superannuation. The contribution rate started at 3 percent, and was increased gradually to 9 percent by 2002.

Superannuation guarantee contributions are a type of concessional contribution and count towards your annual concessional contribution limit. These payments are not designed to provide a full retirement benefit, and it is important to do your own retirement planning on top of this. The reason behind this legislation was to ensure that people could have some retirement benefit put aside, to relieve the dependence on the age pension. These payments are tax deductible for the employer, and taxable to the super fund.

Taxable contributions attract a 15 percent contributions tax. For example, if your employer makes a $1,000 contribution to super on your behalf, then $150 (15 percent) will be paid in tax by the superannuation fund. Your superannuation fund will then invest the remaining $850 into your chosen investments.

How Can I Make Concessional Contributions to Super? Generally, all employer contributions including SGC are concessional contributions. If you are an employee, and your employer is making contributions to super on your behalf, then usually you cannot claim a tax deduction on personal contributions to super.

However, you can get your employer to make contributions for you from your salary. These are known as *salary sacrifice* contributions. For example, if you are earning $5,000 per month as salary, you can ask your employer to reduce your salary to $4,000 per month, and contribute the other $1,000 to super on your behalf. This is an effective way of getting money into super without paying income tax on the contributions.

Beware   There is one thing you need to be aware of before you commence salary sacrifice.

Employers, by law, are only required to pay the 9 percent SGC on your taxable salary, that is, they are not required to pay the 9 percent SGC on any amounts salary sacrificed to superannuation. In the above example where the salary is $60,000, the SGC amount paid to super for the employee would be $5,400.

$$\$60,000 \times 9\% = \$5,400$$

If you salary sacrifice $1,000 per month, then your annual salary is reduced by $12,000

$$\$1,000 \times 12 \text{ months} = \$12,000$$

This then brings your salary to $48,000.

$$\$60,000 - \$12,000 = \$48,000$$

Your employer then has the right to reduce your employer superannuation contributions from $5,400 to $4,320.

$$\$48,000 \times 9\% = \$4,320$$

Many employers will agree to pay the 9 percent on the original $60,000, and you should ask your employer what they will do before you make a decision. You will still be better off (in this example) after salary sacrifice, but you need to know all the facts before making a decision.

Self-Employed Contributions   You can also make concessional contributions to superannuation if you are (a) self-employed, (b) substantially self-employed or (c) have no employer making super contributions for you, such as if you are unemployed or retired (and still eligible to contribute). You are counted as self employed if you are working for yourself as a sole trader or in a partnership. You are considered substantially self-employed, if you receive less than 10 percent of your income from employment. In the past, salary sacrifice superannuation contributions could be used to bring your employment income down to less than 10 percent of your total income. From 1st July, 2009, this is no longer the case.

This last point (c) is important. Let's say you have just come into a windfall. You decide that you no longer need to work, and you are still eligible to contribute to super, as you are under age 65. You can, in any financial year that you have not received employer contributions, make contributions to superannuation, even though you are not working.

If you are a business owner operating under a company structure, your company can make tax deductible contributions to superannuation on your behalf. Whilst this is similar to the previous methods, your company may be able to employ other family members, and thereby provide deductible contributions to super for them. Of course, starting a company is only worthwhile if you intend to conduct some form of business, and is not recommended just to wash through super contributions. The company will need to be earning income from conducting a business (not investment income) before you can use this strategy. Once again, the individual circumstances are the key, and this is where advice is essential.

Tax on Contributions   Any concessional (deductible) contributions to super are taxed at 15 percent (up to the concessional contributions limit) once they are received by the super fund. When you make a contribution, you need to declare whether you are going to claim a tax deduction or not. If you are going to claim a deduction, then this must be taxed by the fund. Let's use the previous example.

You make your contribution of $1,000 as a salary sacrifice contribution. Your employer declares to the receiving super fund that you are doing this as salary sacrifice, and therefore not paying income tax on the money (concessional contribution). The receiving super fund will then set aside 15 percent ($150) of the money you contribute, and this will be paid to the Australian Taxation Office (ATO). Your net contribution is then $850.

Let's use another example, where someone earning $15,000 wishes to salary sacrifice $1,000 per month ($12,000 per annum) to superannuation. This person may have a spouse earning enough to support the family, and so feels that this is a good way to increase their superannuation. As there is no tax paid on the first $6,000 income, this person will only save tax on $9,000, even though they are contributing $12,000.

$$\$15,000 - \$6,000 = \$9,000$$

If only $9,000 is taxable, and the tax rate is 15 cents on the dollar, then the personal tax saving is $1,350.

$$\$9,000 \times \$0.15 = \$1,350 \text{ tax saved}$$

As the whole $12,000 is a salary sacrifice contribution, then when the receiving super fund sets aside money for the ATO, it will do the following calculation:

$$\$12,000 \times 15\% = \$1,800 \text{ tax paid}$$

This means that the tax saving of $1,350 is $450 less than the tax which is paid inside the super fund. This is not an effective strategy, as it has left the employee worse off that before the contribution to super. For this reason, it is always important to obtain advice, as there are many traps for the unadvised.

It is important to be aware that any contributions over the concessional contributions limit are taxed at the top marginal rate, which is 46.5 percent. This can be another trap, as excess contributions will never work in your favour.

Tax on Withdrawal from Superannuation   There is lump sum withdrawal tax to pay on concessional contributions and any investment return on your superannuation, if you withdraw prior to age 60. Below is a table showing what the various rates of superannuation tax payable under the different conditions of withdrawal. The tax rates shown include Medicare levy.

PAYG Withholding Obligations for Funds Paying Lump Sum Benefits

Age of member	Tax free component*	Taxable component**
60 years and over	The entire payment is tax-free after a member turns 60 and funds are not required to withhold any tax from a payment, or issue a payment summary.	
Preservation age but under 60	No tax withheld.	Amount up to low rate cap*** – no tax withheld. Amount above low rate cap – withhold tax at the rate of 16.5%
Below preservation age#	No tax withheld.	Withhold tax at the rate of 21.5%

Source: www.ato.gov.au

*Tax free component is any superannuation contributions which do not attract contributions tax, e.g. non concessional contributions, CGT rollover contributions (on sale of business)

**Taxable component is any contribution on which contributions tax has been paid, and any investment returns earned by the fund

***low rate cap is $150,000 for 2009–2010 financial year

#Preservation age is the age at which once retired, you can withdraw money from superannuation. This may vary according to your date of birth.

If a member does not provide their tax file number before the payment is made, tax is withheld at the rate of 46.5 percent from the taxable component. No tax is withheld where the member has a terminal medical condition and applies for a lump sum super payment.

Non-Concessional Contributions   These were formerly known as undeducted contributions. This is where you contribute to superannuation, without claiming a tax deduction. This is really important for windfall recipients, as many windfalls are not taxable when first received. This means that there is a perfect opportunity for you to put some serious money into super, and get some fabulous benefits along the way.

In the previous section, I spoke about tax on contributions, and tax on withdrawals. This does not apply to non-concessional contributions. (See tax free component in the above table.) So, if you have a windfall and want to get some serious bang for your buck, this is the way to do it. I mentioned before that you can contribute up to $450,000 of non-concessional contributions in one year. In the case of a couple receiving a windfall, then this amount becomes $900,000 ($450,000 each). Of course, there are restrictions on when you can start using the money, (see detailed explanation in Chapter 8) so for a young couple with a windfall of $1,000,000, this would probably be a poor decision, as they would then not have access to the money for years, and would receive no immediate benefit from it.

Total and Permanent Disability (TPD) Payments from Superannuation   This is a situation where, whilst it may be exciting to have the windfall as it provides some degree of financial security which may not have otherwise been available, the circumstances in which it arrives are not happy.

Total and permanent disability is one of the conditions of release for superannuation.

Superannuation Industry (Supervision) Act 1993 (SIS) regulation 6.01(2) defines permanent incapacity, in relation to a member, to mean "ill-health (whether physical or mental), where the trustee is reasonably satisfied that the member is unlikely, because of the ill-health, to engage in gainful employment for which the member is reasonably qualified by education, training or experience".

Whilst a young person may not have built up a significant amount of superannuation, there may be TPD insurance within the superannuation fund, which can provide a substantial benefit.

As an example, a young person with a highly paid job may have insurance of say $1,000,000, and only $35,000 in actual superannuation benefits. On the total and permanent disability of that person, at least $1,000,000 would be paid out. It is possible that $1,035,000 would be paid, depending on whether the insurance was written as a guaranteed payout of $1,000,000 (including the investment balance of $35,000) or whether it was to be paid on top of the investment balance.

As you get older, you are more likely to have a higher investment balance, and higher insurance, as generally the need for insurance increases with age as both income and debts usually increase (at least up to a point—insurance may decrease once commitments such as a mortgage is paid off and any children have left home).

It is important to get advice before you take any TPD insurance from superannuation. It is possible that this may be paid in the form of a superannuation pension, which may be more tax effective than taking it out as a lump sum. Lump sum withdrawal tax is payable on your TPD benefit, but the tax is calculated differently from other lump sums. The tax free component is modified for a disability lump sum.

The tax-free component of a disability lump sum benefit is calculated as the sum of the tax-free component as shown in previous table, and a portion of the taxable amount, determined by using the following formula:

Amount of benefit	×	Days to retirement /
		Service days + Days to retirement

Days to retirement is the number of days from the day on which the member stopped being capable of being gainfully employed to his or her last retirement day (usually age 65) and *Service days* is the number of days in the service period for the lump sum.

Source: www.ato.gov.au

The result of the above formula is that someone taking their superannuation as a payment under total and permanent disability will get a higher tax free amount than would otherwise be available. The closer you are to retirement, the smaller the extra tax free component will be.

BENEFITS FROM SUPERANNUATION FOR SPECIFIC WINDFALLS

Superannuation and Inheritance An inheritance from the deceased's superannuation fund can provide benefits to certain beneficiaries in the form of a tax free lump sum, or a tax effective pension. This will be discussed in detail in the chapters on estate planning and pensions, but a couple of points are important to note. Lump sums are only tax free if paid to a tax dependant (including a spouse or minor or financially dependent child).

Superannuation pensions which are left to a spouse or dependent child under age 25 as a reversionary pension (that means, they can keep the pension and its tax benefits, even if they are not eligible for a pension themselves), are a great tax planning tool that can be set up for the beneficiaries by the deceased. This should not be treated lightly, and is probably best left as a pension rather than withdrawn. It is important to seek advice before you make a decision if you are in receipt of a reversionary pension.

Robert and Anne came to see me after Robert was diagnosed with a terminal illness. Robert wanted to know how best to provide for Anne with the money that was to be paid to him as a terminal illness benefit from his superannuation. I advised him to commence an allocated pension for himself, and nominate Anne as the reversionary beneficiary. Anne was not eligible to receive a superannuation pension in her own name, as she was only 48 at the time. By taking my advice, Robert was able to leave Anne with a tax free income which would have been otherwise unavailable to her. Many years later she is still benefiting from Robert's consideration for her during what must have been a terrible time.

Superannuation and Sale of a Business   There are a number of concessions which are designed to reduce the capital gains tax paid on the sale of a small business. Superannuation plays a role, as there is the ability to put up to $1,100,000 from the sale of the business (if the business is subject to the 15 year exemption from capital gains tax) in to super. This is not taxed when it goes into super (non-concessional contribution) and it also is not taxed as a capital gain.

Superannuation will also help you if you have owned your business for less than 15 years. For example, let's say you sold your business for $1,000,000 more than it cost you. This means that you have a capital gain of $1,000,000. This will give you a taxable capital gain of $500,000 after the 50 percent CGT discount, and by applying the small business CGT discount you will bring your taxable capital gain down to $250,000. You can elect to pay $250,000 of this gain into super, and then there will be no tax to pay on this money—no contributions tax (15 percent) and no capital gains tax. Please see Chapter 6 for further information on the tax treatment of a business sale.

At the beginning of this chapter, I mentioned that superannuation is a complex matter and that professional advice is a must. I have given you a simple overview of the most common ways of using superannuation to make the best use of your windfall.

SUMMARY

- Superannuation is a method of providing for your retirement, whilst at the same time legally minimising tax.
- Contributions to super may be tax deductible.
- Tax on earnings inside superannuation is at 15 percent, lower than most people's marginal rate of tax.
- Tax on lump sums from super may be tax free.
- You may be able to contribute to super (and claim a tax deduction), even if you are not working.
- Superannuation has extra benefits for some windfall events (inheritance, sale of business, and total and permanent disability).

- Superannuation is complex, and it is important to get professional advice in this area.

Next we look at how you can reduce the tax on your income, not only in retirement, but whilst you are still working. And when I say reduce your tax, I mean potentially to zero. Even if you are not close to retirement, this chapter will show you why superannuation is so important to your financial planning.

CHAPTER 8

How Can I Minimise Tax on My Retirement Income?

At first glance, this chapter may not seem all that relevant to you. You may be 30 years old and have just won the lottery. It is still important, in that it explains the reasons that superannuation is important, at any age. You are setting yourself up for the long term use of your wealth, not only for your own retirement, but also for future generations. So you need to know what you are planning for, and how it will help you, not only now, but in the future, as well.

This chapter is not just for the "oldies." If you are 50 or over, it is probably the most important chapter in the book. It is also relevant for those who have been paid out under total and permanent disability insurance, and possibly for those who have had compensation claims. It may also be extremely relevant if you have had an inheritance, particularly if it was from a spouse, or someone who supported you financially. So read on and enjoy. Contained in this chapter are the rewards for not relying on taxpayers to support you once you are no longer working.

First, I shall go through the various "conditions of release" of superannuation. That's financial planning jargon for when you can get money from your super. It's only when you get your money out of super that the real benefits start. This is when you can take an income from your superannuation, and possibly even have a superannuation pension, whilst you are still working, and not eligible to withdraw your super. If this all sounds confusing, then remember that this is the new "simpler super" system!

There are three super benefit categories:

- unrestricted non-preserved
- restricted non-preserved
- preserved

Unrestricted non-preserved benefits can be taken out at any time, as they are not subject to *preservation* rules. These are generally contributions made in the early nineties or earlier, prior to the preservation rules being announced.

Restricted non-preserved benefits can be taken out once you have ceased work with the employer who contributed to the fund.

Preserved benefits must meet a condition of release. The conditions of release are:

- Retirement after attaining preservation age
  (see below)
- Turning 65
- Death
- Total and permanent disability
  (from any occupation)
- Terminal illness
- Financial hardship
- Compassionate grounds
- Change of employers after age 60
- Employment has ceased and the benefit is under $200
- You are a "lost member" and the benefit is under $200
- Temporary residents departing Australia
- You can access pension benefits whilst still working
  using the "transition to retirement" provisions,
  once you have reached preservation age.

I shall now go through the details on each of the above points, as "the devil is in the detail," as my friend, Katrina, says.

Retirement   This is when you cease to become gainfully employed after attaining preservation age. See below.

Date of birth	Preservation age
Before 1 July 1960	55
1 July 1960 – 30 June 1961	56
1 July 1961 – 30 June 1962	57
1 July 1962 – 30 June 1963	58
1 July 1963 – 30 June 1964	59
From 1 July 1964	60

Source: www.ato.gov.au

You also must not intend to start work again. This is an interesting point that is often questioned by my clients. How do you measure intention? The simple answer is that you can't. It could be argued, however, that someone who retires on Friday and starts work again on Monday probably didn't intend to retire.

My father retired due to a series of health issues in 1986. A couple of months later, he was asked by his employer of 43 years to return to work on a consultancy basis for about six weeks. After this was completed and he had resumed retirement, he was asked to return to work at least twice. Preservation rules didn't exist in 1986, so it was not relevant that he went back to work, but here is a case of someone who clearly intended to retire, but at a quick glance, it may appear not to be the case. I am pleased to report that he has been in excellent health for the last 23 years. Retirement obviously agrees with him.

Turning 65   Once you turn 65, your super is yours regardless of whether you are working or not. This is probably the simplest of the conditions of release.

Death   This results in the release of super, but it does have a little-known trick to it. When contributions tax was introduced in 1988, there was a provision written into the Income Tax Assessment Act (ITAA section 279D) which allowed for any contributions tax paid by the deceased to be paid back to the beneficiaries. This is because death benefits are tax free. The benefit needs to be still in superannuation (not pension) to claim the full benefit. For someone who has been in pension phase for a short time, there may still be some benefit available.

This is known as the "anti-detriment" provision. Unfortunately, there is no law that says that this must be paid to the beneficiaries by the super fund. Some pay it automatically, whilst others hope that the beneficiaries are not aware of it, and hold on to it until it is requested.

Total and Permanent Disability   This may seem simple enough, and it would be if there weren't two definitions of TPD. One is known as the "own occupation" definition. This means that if you can no longer perform your own occupation (e.g., teacher) then you can claim on your TPD policy. The other is the "any occupation" definition. This means you are unable to perform any occupation for which you are reasonably suited by education, training, or experience.

Superannuation legislation uses the "any occupation" definition. So, if you are paid out under an "own occupation" policy held by a superannuation fund, and are not totally and permanently disabled under the definition in the legislation, then your benefit will stay in super until a condition of release is met.

Terminal Illness   If you have a terminal illness, you can apply for your superannuation benefit regardless of your age. It may depend on the rules of the super fund as to whether this is available to you.

Financial Hardship and Compassionate Grounds   These are not easy methods by which to access superannuation. They involve application to APRA (Australian Prudential Regulation Authority) and may often result in a small portion of the benefit being paid to you. For financial hardship, you need to have been in receipt of Centrelink support for at least 26 weeks, and show inability to meet necessary personal expenses. These restrictions are relaxed if you are 39 weeks over your preservation age.

Janne Ashton

Change of Employers After Age 60   If you leave an employer after age 60, you are deemed to be retired, even if you get another job.

Benefits under $200   These apply to super funds from previous employers. If the benefit is under $200, and there are no contributions going into the fund, then you can withdraw your superannuation. Bear in mind that you will pay tax on the benefit, so you will actually get less than $200. You are considered a "lost member" if the super fund does not have your current contact details.

Temporary Residents Departing Australia   You need to be leaving Australia permanently to be able to take your superannuation, and this will be taxed more heavily than if you were using another condition of release.

Super and Divorce   In 2001, changes to the Family Law legislation allowed that superannuation can be divided by an agreement or court order, in the case of marriage breakdown.

Transition to Retirement   I shall discuss this in detail later in this chapter.

RETIREMENT INCOME

Superannuation Pensions   This is the exciting bit, and where the true rewards are. In the past in Australia, superannuation was taken as a lump sum by most people. It was then invested or spent, according to the needs and the nature of the retiree.

Once governments started to focus on the aging baby boomers and the potential drain on Australian society if they all required social security support, then legislation was used to change the attitude of retirees.

Legislation initially focused on punishment (by way of tax) for those who wanted a lump sum, by taxing their benefit at

30 percent (above a tax free threshold). This was later changed to 15 percent, with a contributions tax of 15 percent, as well. Whilst mathematically this makes no difference to the end benefit, it brought forward the time at which the tax was collected, giving the tax office a great boost to its income.

There was also a reasonable benefits limit (RBL), which meant that if you had "too much" super, then the tax rate went up to the top marginal rate at the time.

On 1st July, 2007, the new "simpler super" system was introduced. This took away much of the tax on lump sums, and used the carrot instead of the stick. The RBL was removed, and any money taken from super after age 60 was tax free, on either lump sums or pensions. Tax free! After approximately 40 years of paying tax, suddenly no more tax. That is, if your money is in super. You can take it out tax free, but then when you invest it, you will pay tax. But if you leave it in the super system, then your income is tax free.

For most people, their biggest budget item is tax, although it is not recognised, as it has usually been taken out prior to receiving their income (PAYG). When your biggest expense has gone, then it leaves a lot more to spend. So the issue for Australians now is not how to get money out of super, but how to get it into super prior to retirement.

The new simpler super policy included restrictions on how much you could contribute to super. So, when you get your windfall, this has to be one of the most important parts of your financial plan. If you are young, then an annual contribution will set you up well for a decent tax free income in retirement. If you are 50 or over, (not that that's old, even though my boys like to tell me different) then it is imperative that you get advice on retirement planning, as this will be your most effective investment.

Superannuation Pensions A super pension is just an income that comes from super. These are also referred to as "income streams," or retirement income. To qualify for the tax benefits

Janne Ashton

that apply to superannuation pensions, the superannuation benefit must be "rolled over" to the pension. Rolling over means super is moved directly to the pension. This is vital, as once it has come out of super; you may not be able to get it back into super.

Allocated Pensions These are the most common form of super pension. The term "allocated" refers to the fact that an account is allocated to your name, and that you have access to the balance of that account. The balance of that account may rise and fall, according to the amount of withdrawals and the performance of the fund (positive or negative). You cannot add to an *allocated pension*, but you can have multiple allocated pensions.

You can choose the amount of income you would like in an allocated pension. There are minimum amounts that you have to take, and these are based on your age. The minimum if you are under age 65 is 4 percent, and it goes to 14 percent by age 95. Income is adjusted on 1 July each year, according to your account balance and your age. If your account balance has increased, then your pension income will increase. If your account balance has decreased, your income may fall, or it may increase if you have reached an age where the percentage has increased (say, from 4 to 5 percent).

This means that the income you choose is unrelated to either the income or growth of the fund. For example, if you choose a 5 percent income, and the superannuation fund consistently earns 7 percent, then your balance will be increasing each year by the amount of the unused return. If the income you choose is 10 percent (you can choose to have more than the minimum) then you will have a falling account balance.

Below is a table showing the minimum income based on age. Minimum pension incomes for each financial year are calculated on 1 July, based on both the account balance and the relevant percentage based on age of the pension owner at that time.

Age	Minimum Withdrawal as a % of the Account Balance
Under 65	4%
65–74	5%
75–79	6%
80–84	7%
85–89	9%
90–94	11%
95 or more	14%

One of my clients, Des, retired at age 65. He and his wife, Annette, are (and have always been) very prudent and intelligent with their money. Des told me how much income they required, and I set about putting a financial plan together for him. When he came to see me to discuss his plan, I advised him that he would have to take more income than he required, as his desired income was under the minimum amount. It's not a problem that a lot of people have, but he had over the years built up a huge super balance. Des and Annette regularly have a lovely holiday overseas, and this is easily affordable with their income.

Annuities   These are retirement incomes that can be purchased using a lump sum. You often give up access to your lump sum in return for a guaranteed income for the rest of your life, however long that may be. You can have a reversionary benefit to a spouse, and the amount of income you receive will be determined by the life expectancy of both you and (if applicable) your spouse.

Pensions for People Under Age 60   If you are under age 60 and getting a pension from your superannuation, then there are some fabulous tax advantages for you. This applies to those who have been able to access their super early. In the case of Windfall Club members, this is most likely for those who have been paid a TPD benefit, or a compensation claim for a total and permanent disability.

We can classify your superannuation into two parts: the taxed and the tax free portions. They are treated differently when you commence a pension, and so you need to know the difference. The tax free component is the sum of your personal or non tax deductible contributions. This includes all non-concessional contributions, small business rollover, and the invalidity component of a TPD benefit. So if you have a tax free component of, say, $500,000, then any pension from this will be tax free.

The balance of your superannuation, (the taxed portion) when taken as a pension, is taxable to you but will attract a tax rebate of 15 percent. In the example below, we look at how much tax you will pay on a super pension as compared to ordinary (non super) income. In the example, I have assumed a benefit of $1,000,000, with $500,000 tax free component and $500,000 taxed component. I am also assuming that you have chosen an income of 6 percent, and that you have $6,000 income from another source.

Income from tax free component:

$500,000 × 6% = $30,000

Income from taxed component:

$500,000 × 6% = $30,000

Total income: $60,000 plus $6,000 = $66,000

Tax on tax free component: Nil

Tax on taxed component plus $6,000 other income:

$36,000 taxed at current marginal rates: $4,650
15% rebate on $30,000 = $4,500
$4,650 − $4,500 = $150 tax on income.

Had this been taxed as ordinary income, you would have paid $13,650 tax, plus Medicare levy of $990. So you have an income of over $280 per week extra, because you have put some (or all) of your windfall into superannuation. Think of what you can do with an extra $280 a week.

Pensions for People Age 60 and Over   This is simple. If you are 60 or over, and commence a superannuation pension, you pay no tax on the income. Nil, zero, zip, nothing! If you think this is exciting, read on and find out how you can also do this on your salary whilst you are still working.

Transition to Retirement   The "transition to retirement" legislation came about to suit people who wanted to semi-retire. Because of the preservation rules, people found it difficult to reduce their working hours as they got older, as they could not subsidise their income from their superannuation.

To alleviate this problem, legislation passed in 2005 allowed people who have reached their preservation age to take a pension from their superannuation, even if they are still working. This meant that those who wanted to semi-retire could now access their super to support their income. The maximum amount payable each financial year is 10 percent of the value of the super (which has been commuted to a pension).

The advantage for everyone over preservation age soon became apparent. Income can be salary sacrificed to super, and the super rolled over to provide a pension. Whilst this is an advantage for every working person over preservation age, the real winners are the 60 and over age group.

A friend of mine, Ken, who was over 60, was earning around $110,000 per annum. I asked him to come and see me, as I had something I wished to discuss with him. When he came to my office, I explained transition to retirement. I had a spreadsheet that calculates the benefit of this strategy and, in his case, his income tax was reduced by $25,000 per annum. How is this possible?

He pays income tax at marginal rates, and the result is a total income tax payment of $30,000 annum. By salary sacrificing some of his salary to superannuation, he can reduce this income tax from $30,000 to $5,000 per annum. Because the amount he can take as a pension is limited to 10 percent of his superannuation balance, he could not get rid of all his income tax, only $25,000 of it.

As he is over 60, the tax on his pension from superannuation is also zero. So he has just gotten rid of his tax, or most of it. He will still have to pay 15 percent tax on his salary sacrifice contributions to super. He wasn't too concerned about that, because the other sweetener is that now that his super is in a pension, he no longer has to pay 15 percent tax on the earnings of the fund, as pension returns are tax free.

He was able to use the extra $25,000 to increase his super balance. This is because I explained how much pension benefit he will need to give him the same after tax income that he had before. As he now needs to take $25,000 less, because he doesn't have to pay tax, he can leave that money in his super fund, and retire wealthier. From 1st July 2009, he has had to slightly reduce his salary sacrifice, as the concessional contributions limit has reduced. This has had a minor impact on his benefits from the strategy, and he is still much better off than he was before.

Of course, you can also use this technique to increase your take home pay, or do a bit of both—some extra super, some extra pay. It is up to you, and completely legal.

SUMMARY

- You can withdraw money from superannuation once you meet a condition of release.
- The most common conditions of release are:
  - retirement at or after preservation age
  - attaining age 65
  - change of employers after age 60
  - total and permanent disability
  - death
- Superannuation pensions provide fabulous tax advantages, and are tax free for everyone once they have had their 60th birthday.

- Superannuation pensions may be tax free or partially tax free if you are under age 60.
- You can access your superannuation as a pension (with all the above tax advantages) when you have reached preservation age, even if you are still working.

After you have completed your financial plan, and minimised your tax on your income, you may feel that you are in a position to spend some money on yourself, or give some money to family or friends. We next look at some ideas for you to consider before making any decisions, so that you can get maximum pleasure from spending and giving.

CHAPTER 9

Spending and Giving

I find many people, when presented with a large sum of money, are quite diligent in getting rid of it. This may be because, subconsciously, they don't believe they deserve it, or they don't really want it. We all have different attitudes towards money, and those that have a positive outlook on financial success are much more likely to achieve it. A negative attitude towards money may be an underlying cause of financial failure, even after having received a windfall.

Spending and giving can be the two greatest pleasures that a windfall has to offer. They can also be the undoing of some windfall recipients, especially those who believe that money is the root of all evil. We all believe that we enjoy money, and very few of us consciously believe that we don't want it. It all happens at a deeper level, and if our core beliefs are that wealth is bad, then we will seek to rid ourselves of wealth.

Below are some sayings that I believe show a negative attitude towards money. All these comments are appropriate at times, but if you find yourself using comments such as these on a regular basis, you will need to be on the lookout for destructive financial habits.

- "Money is the root of all evil."
- "Rich bastard."
- "Knowing my luck, (some disaster will occur)."
- "I would have been rich, but (someone else's fault)."
- "I hate rich people."
- "I'm working-class and proud of it."
- "Look at (some celebrity). All the money in the world and they are still not happy."

- "Money can't buy happiness."
- "Rich people have so many problems."
- "Having all this money has created such a lot of problems"

Most of the sayings above are true, at least some of the time. But if they (or other negative sayings about money) are a part of your conversation reasonably regularly, the underlying message that you are giving yourself is that you are better off without money. Do this often enough and you will believe it.

Be on the lookout for negative comments about money. They may be completely different from those above, but if you believe money is bad, negative comments about money are likely to be part of your language. If you receive a windfall, you won't want to be like those (evil, unhappy, unlucky, upper-class, bastard) rich people, so you will seek to rid yourself of the problem—the money. A psychologist or NLP practitioner will be able to help you eradicate any negative attitude to money or wealth.

Spending is one of the joys of a windfall. Instead of working hard to pay the bills and spending the bit that is left (which is usually a small portion of your total income), you suddenly have the ability to spend, without using your hard-earned income. No wonder many people become extravagant in their spending. Here is the chance that we have all hoped for; to own the things that we could never afford.

Of course, if you spend too much, then the financial freedom that a windfall can bring may never eventuate. Out of control spending usually ends in disaster, and on many occasions, disaster is not only the loss of the money, but also loss of previously owned (pre-windfall) assets. Let me give you some examples.

In a conversation earlier this week, I was told of a colleague who had bought a house (a mansion, really) for $1,500,000. This mansion had everything you could ever dream of in a house. It was on acreage in Sydney, and was absolutely magnificent. Although the house was a few years old, the kitchen appeared to be virtually brand new. This was because the previous owners (lottery winners) had bought take-away every night. They had never cooked.

My son, Lee, always says that he will know we are rich when we can afford our own chef! It sounds like a dream; never having to cook again, but clearly, the previous owners couldn't afford that lifestyle, as they had to sell their house, which had cost them $3,000,000 to build (including land). They were no longer working, and needed some money to live on.

There are some obvious mistakes that people make that show that they are on the path to financial destruction. Hints that your spending may be out of control include the following:

- Buying an expensive item, and then deciding you no longer want it (e.g., car) then buying another one, after selling the previous item at a massive loss
- Becoming the person that everyone comes to for money
- Lavish overseas holidays (many of them)
- Gambling
- More than one business failure
- Not investing at all; just spending
- Not getting professional advice
- Getting involved in highly risky enterprises
- Forgetting to insure valuable items
- Becoming a shopaholic and having a collection of unopened items at home, or giving away things that you have recently bought because you no longer want or need them
- Any spending without thought as to the financial consequences

This last point is very telling. If you think you can spend without ever considering whether you can afford it, you are probably out of control. You may have a windfall of several million dollars, but that will run out, too, if you overspend. There is always a limit to a windfall, unless it is providing you with income. Then it can go on forever, if you only spend the income. You may also find yourself making excuses for your spending. Excuses, to me, are always a warning sign that things are not going well.

Emotional Spending   As I mentioned earlier, the windfall recipients all go through extreme emotions. We have two methods of making decisions—emotional and rational. Emotional decisions are made to satisfy some emotional need, rather than a practical one. It may be that we just want an item, even if it is not really affordable or useful. Emotional decisions are not always bad, because we usually only make emotional decisions occasionally, and generally when we have a limited spending capacity. Rational decisions are those where we consider the options and the positives and negatives of each option, and then decide what is best for us. Most decisions are a mix of the two, with one more dominant.

The car that I am driving at the moment was a predominantly emotional purchase. I was doing a loan for a client who worked in a car dealership. I was very happy with the car I was driving at the time, but when I saw this beautiful yellow car (my favourite colour) I had to have it. It was not as practical as the car I already had, but to me it was, and still is, the prettiest car on the road. There was of course some rational thought in place. The car was affordable, comfortable, had low mileage and was also economical to run, all of which were important to me as I am a frequent driver.

When I was visiting my friend, Diane recently, I met Cameron. When Cameron had gone through an emotionally difficult time, she relieved her stress by shopping. Her house was filled with unopened books and CDs, many of which she had multiple copies. She would just go out and buy things to make herself feel better, even though she would never use them. This is emotional spending without any rational thought. By the time I met Cameron, she was well past this period and had gotten rid of her collection of unwanted goods.

The problem with making chiefly emotional decisions after receipt of a windfall is that for most people, there has been no experience with this much money or this much emotion—certainly not both together. This makes for bad decisions.

Giving is another pleasure. Nothing can be more gratifying than to help out a friend or family member and see them prosper as a result. I love to give, as do most people. It is often a greater pleasure to give than receive. Keep in mind, though, that your gift of money may not be treated with the respect you believe it deserves. How would you feel if you gave a friend $50,000 and they blew it at the casino in one night? It may destroy the friendship. So, be very selective about the amount you give away, and about the recipients of your gifts.

There are other pressures that can cause issues for you after you have had a windfall. Your friends may expect you to pay, not occasionally but every time they go out for dinner or to some form of entertainment that costs money. Your friends and family may ask you to pay for something, then "forget" to pay you back. It may be difficult to raise the subject with them, especially if you let it happen a few times.

You may be targeted for loans and gifts, or you may feel that you have to support members of your family and friends with a gift of cash. Many clients have often said, "I would like to pay out my son/daughter's mortgage" or expressed a desire to give them some money. That's very generous. You just need to know if it fits into your budget before you make the decision. Your ability to be generous is directly related to how long your money will last, which will affect your future generosity.

SUMMARY

Spending and giving are two of the great joys of receiving a windfall. To have these pleasures for the rest of your life, you need to watch out for:

- A negative attitude to money
- Out of control (emotional) spending
- Out of control giving

If you are aware of these behaviors:

- If you feel that you have a negative attitude to money, seek advice from a psychologist or NLP practitioner.
- Contact your planner if you can't control your spending.

- Enjoy being generous within your means, and you can be generous for the rest of your life.

In the following chapter, we will look at how to manage your budget for the rest of your life. This will give you the skills needed to ensure that you can enjoy a lifetime of spending and giving.

CHAPTER 10

Managing the "Life Budget"

How many people have ever done a budget and stuck to it religiously? Not many! So why is it important to do a budget now that you have more money than ever before? This is a big part of deciding what you would like to achieve, and also it gives you a guide to follow.

Traditionally, any discussion of budgeting covers short term spending, usually weekly, monthly or yearly. We are told to pay our bills first, save or invest some money for the future and then spend what is left. This is great advice for people on a regular income, as each week, fortnight or month, some more money will turn up and the cycle will repeat.

The bad news for windfall recipients is that for a windfall, it just doesn't work. The reason for this is that short term budgeting does not need to take into account the effects of inflation, changes in tax, interest rates and investment returns. You will need to have access to a budget calculator which can factor in these variables, and thereby provide you with a "life budget". Here are the steps to managing your life budget.

Set goals for your lifestyle   Think of what you would like to do now that you have more money. Would you like to eat out every night, go on two holidays a year, drive an expensive car, give money to your family and friends, live in a mansion, or all of the above? Be specific about your goals and what they will cost. If you would like an annual holiday, estimate the cost based on when and where you are going.

Prioritise your goals   Part of the process of budgeting is prioritising. If you had an unlimited amount of money, you would never need to prioritise, as you would be able to have everything. Even the richest person has a limit to what their money can buy. Once you get into budgeting, you will quickly realise what is most important to you, as you will cut unimportant things from the budget first.

Estimate your expenses   First you will need to add up your entire one off expenses and subtract this amount from your windfall. This will give you the amount that you have left to invest. Once you know what you would like to spend, you can add it all up and then you have a preliminary budget. You will need to add at least 10 percent for things that have been inadvertently left out of your budget – there is always something. Once you know the limit of your budget, it is much easier to stick to it.

Seek advice as to how much of your windfall you will need to invest to maintain your lifestyle   This is where you will need to involve your financial planner. There are so many variables in investing money, and the return you can expect will vary according to your risk profile and the investments you choose. Of course, as the expected return varies, so does the amount of the windfall which needs to be invested.

This also involves deciding whether you need to continue to work at the same level, reduce your work hours, or retire completely. No wonder some people have trouble—they have never been taught to manage their last pay. If you stop work when you receive your windfall, then this is the last pay packet you will ever receive. Yes, it is a big one, but it is still the last. So for you, a different budget calculator is required. You will need a budget calculator that takes into account changes in inflation, tax, lifestyle and investment returns. Over periods of a year or less, these are not so relevant, but if you are budgeting for life, they are essential.

Make allowance for changes in tax, inflation, investment returns and lifestyle   These can all have a massive impact on your budget. For most people, tax is the biggest budget item, so a significant increase in the tax rates may mean that your budget is no longer workable.

Inflation is another risk to your life budget. The present value of your money is much greater than the future value. This is because inflation will deplete the value of you money quickly. Inflation in Australia has averaged about three percent over the last 10 years. That means that if you had a windfall of $1,000,000 ten years ago, then you would now need $1,344,000 to have retained the value of the money.

Let's assume you receive a windfall of $3,000,000 at the age of 40. You expect a return of 5 percent on your money, and after completing a budget, you believe that you can live well on a gross income of $100,000 per annum. You work out that $2,000,000 invested at 5 percent return will give you your $100,000 annual income, and so this leaves you $1,000,000 for one off expenses. After spending the $1,000,000, you are looking forward to a lifetime of comfort. If we assume a 3 percent inflation rate, by the age of 50, you will only be able to spend the equivalent of $73,000 per annum (in today's dollars). By age 60, you are down to $54,000 per annum and at age 70, $40,000—hardly a windfall is it?

Of course, if you invest into some growth assets, then these will grow in value over time to allow you to keep pace with inflation, but changes in tax, lifestyle and investment returns (particularly downturns in markets as in the last couple of years, and changes in interest rates) also need to be factored in to your calculations.

Investment returns are a hot topic at any time, and we often read articles about market falls reducing the value of investments. So is cash a safe alternative? In the late 1980s and early 1990s I was working as a financial planner on the mid north coast of NSW. At that time we had interest rates of around 17 percent. Many people were retiring and moving to the area, and after they had purchased a house, they had about $200,000 to invest. This gave them an income of $34,000 per annum, which was sufficient to live well at that time. By 1993, term deposit rates were down to four percent and their income was down to $8,000. That's a decrease of more than 75 percent of their income.

Those who retired in 2008 had massive decreases in share values, and if they decided to invest in cash as a safe alternative, have seen interest rates fall from over eight percent to around four percent, thereby halving their income. No wonder people find long term budgeting difficult!

Lifestyle may change significantly once you stop work. Weekends and holidays are the times when your discretionary spending is at its highest. Once you retire, you have a permanent weekend/holiday. These are the times that you have time to fill, and shopping, holidays and entertainment are all well used methods of filling this time. That of course, is fine, as long as it is within your budget. Keep in mind, though, that these activities are all expensive and can quickly erode your fortune if they remain unchecked.

Stick to your budget   Once you know the limit of your budget, it is much easier to stick to it. If, for example, you know that you have $8,000 per month to spend, and you start spending $16,000 per month, you know you are on the path to financial ruin. If you can quickly stop this extra spending, then fine. If not, this is the time to pick up the phone and arrange a meeting with your planner.

Don't try to justify it to yourself, as this will not bring the money back once it is gone. This behaviour is probably a sign that your emotions are in charge, rather than your rational self. If you need help with this, then a psychologist is the professional you may wish to call.

Manage your cash flow   Cash flow relates to the timing of expenses. Using the example above, you may have added up all your expenses for the year, and the total is $96,000. This equates to $8,000 per month, so you arrange to have $8,000 per month put into your account to cover your expenses. That should work, shouldn't it? Not necessarily.

Janne Ashton

Let's say you start your budget on 1 July. You will have $8,000 deposited into your account on the first of each month. In August, however, many of your bills fall due. It may be council rates, insurances, car registration and insurance, and your annual holiday. If you need to spend $15,000 in August, you are going to run out of money, as much or all of July's money will be spent by August. It is important to allow for the timing of your expenses. Any good budget will allow for this by using a buffer, which is spare cash to carry through until your next payment.

Your financial plan will include a cash flow analysis, and a budget which is sensitive to your needs. This is based on the original discussions with your planner, and will give you the opportunity to spend at a level which is in line with your current position. A good planner will generally try to improve your financial position over time, rather than deplete it.

If you make a conscious decision to spend more than you earn, then this will be part of your cash flow. This often happens in the case of retirees who often talk about joining the "SKI CLUB". SKI stands for Spend the Kids Inheritance! Many retirees stage a drawdown of their capital over a number of years, generally based on their life expectancy. This allows them to use the wealth they have built over their lifetime to supplement any income that they earn and provides them with a better lifestyle in retirement.

Either way, you need to pay careful attention to your budget, especially in the early stages. A budget is a guide to your spending ability, and should be treated as such. If you have a budget of $10,000 per month, try to go a little under it, as there will be times when you need to spend extra, when you have car troubles or a major appliance breaks down. You may also need to include holidays in this budget, so will need to set aside some money to ensure that you can afford the holiday you had planned.

One simple way to manage your spending is to have an account which you use for everyday spending. Only put money into this account which you are prepared to spend. If you have a budget of $10,000 per month, and will use some of this for one off expenses such as a holiday, then just transfer $8,000 per month to that account, and live off that. The rest of the money can stay in a high interest account until you need it.

Review your budget It is important to review your budget regularly to ensure that you are on track. You can do this yourself, or ask your financial planner to review it with you. You may need to make some adjustments, if you are spending too little or too much, or if your income estimates are not accurate. Tax and inflation will also need to be taken into account as these can change suddenly.

Special note for Sportspeople and Entertainers Most people are advised to live within their means. For you, living beneath your means is a must. You have potentially a short time in which you can set yourself up for life. Some careful planning will allow you to have a fabulous lifestyle now, and at the same time set yourself up for a future where the wealth continues even if the career does not. If you are one of the few who has a long career, then that is great—you will be even wealthier as time goes on, and you can enjoy your wealth in the knowledge that you have set yourself up for life.

SUMMARY

The ability to manage your life budget is one of the most important skills for a windfall recipient. To achieve this, you will need to:

- Set goals for your lifestyle
- Prioritise your goals
- Estimate your expenses
- Seek advice as to how much you need to invest to maintain your lifestyle
- Make allowance for changes in tax, inflation, investment returns and lifestyle
- Stick to your budget
- Manage your cash flow

- Review your budget
- Sports people and entertainers need to live beneath their means.

In the next chapter, we look at another component to a financial plan: debt management. You may feel that you are now in a position to rid yourself of debt, and that is great. It is still important to know some of the tips and traps with loans, and the right advice may save you lots of money.

CHAPTER 11

What About My Loans?

Debt management is something that is essential to cash flow planning. For most people, their loan repayments are the largest item on their budget, other than tax. Debts can be divided into two groups: non-tax deductible (bad) debt and tax deductible (good) debt.

Non-Tax Deductible Debt The most common form of non-deductible debt is a mortgage on your own home. Because your own home does not produce assessable income (income which is assessable for income tax), then the interest paid on the mortgage is not tax deductible. If you have a flat that you rent out which is part of your home, or use it for a home office, then the proportion of the home that produces assessable income can be used to claim a tax deduction. For example, if 20 percent of the area of the house is used to produce assessable income, then 20 percent of the interest on the mortgage may be tax deductible.

Another commonly held investment that does not attract a tax deduction on the interest is a residential block of land. As this does not produce income, then interest is not tax deductible. This may also be the case for rural land, although this can be used to produce income even without a building on it. Examples are if it is used for agistment or cultivation. Interest on car loans and credit cards are not tax deductible, unless used for business purposes.

We call this bad debt because the interest on loans for these investments is not tax deductible. This debt is expensive, especially for those on high incomes, which includes most windfall recipients. You will have to pay tax on your income, and then pay the interest with what is left over after tax. If you are on the top tax rate (46.5 percent including Medicare levy), this is a very expensive proposition.

It is important to note that any principal repayments (repaying the loan itself) are not tax deductible. It is only the interest that may be deductible.

Whilst it will probably be recommended that you pay off your non-deductible debt (if you have sufficient funds from your windfall), you will not always be advised to get rid of the loan. You may use the loan for further investment, and save yourself a lot of money in fees, and a lot of bother. It is always best to get advice when it comes to your finances.

Tax Deductible Debt   Debt is tax deductible when it is used to purchase an asset that will produce assessable income. Examples of this are investments in shares, property, or a business. We call this good debt, because you are paying interest with pre tax dollars.

Say, for example, you have an income of $100,000. You purchase a property for $500,000, and borrow $400,000. You are paying 7 percent interest. Your interest cost is therefore $28,000 per annum. This interest will be deducted from your income, leaving you with a taxable income after deduction of $72,000. Of course, once the property is rented, then the rent will add on to your income. If the rent is $15,000, then your taxable income based on your interest cost and rental income will be $87,000.

$$\$100,000 + \$15,000 - \$28,000 = \$87,000.$$

If you have a fairly complex debt position, you will need some specialist advice, and may need to involve a mortgage broker. Mortgage brokers can search for the best loan for you from a large number of lenders, including the major banks, and a number of smaller lenders. Because they are paid a commission by the lender, there is usually no charge to you for their service and advice.

It is best to involve your financial planner in the process, as they can advise you on how to structure your loans for the best result according to your goals and current position. The mortgage broker will be able to choose the best loan, and this will vary according to which features are important to you. There is such a huge array of loans available these days, with many different features, and there is quite an art to matching the right loan for the client's needs.

My niece, Lindsay, wanted to buy her first home. She and her boyfriend Nick, were both working. The catch was that Nick was on a six-month contract, and had only worked full-time for one month (prior to that he had been a student) and Lindsay was partially self-employed and partly an employee. As she didn't have her tax returns up to date, we could only use the employee income in the loan application. I found a lender who approved their application, but it is unlikely that they would have found a loan themselves, as they did not fit the lending criteria of the major banks. As a broker, I could find out easily which lender had the best chance of approving the loan, without leaving my desk. This saved them a lot of running around and potential disappointment.

Your financial planner can advise you on how to structure your loans for the best result according to your goals and your current position. I had a client, Joshua, who saw me on the insistence of a friend of his who was already my client. He was reluctant to see me because he was having trouble managing his budget after a decrease in the family income, and he didn't think I would be able to help. As I am a licensed mortgage broker as well as a financial planner, I had a look at his debts and quickly saw that I could improve his cash flow position.

I used the following plan of action:

• Changed his home loan to interest only
• Found another lender with a much lower interest rate, and low fees
• Consolidated his credit card debt and car loan into his housing loan

Janne Ashton

The effect of this was that after I had also recommended appropriate insurances for him, his cash flow improved by nearly $20,000! He was delighted. Some of his cash flow improvement was brought about by making his loan interest only, but this did not disadvantage him, as on one hand he was reducing debt on his housing loan, and on the other hand he was increasing debt on his credit card. This is not a winning strategy.

SUMMARY

- Debt can be considered good if the interest is tax deductible and bad if the interest is not tax deductible.
- You will need advice from your financial planner as to what action to take with regard to your debt.
- You may need the help of a mortgage broker, who can advise you on the best loan for your situation.

We will now look at how you can use insurance as a low cost method to protect both your income and your assets.

CHAPTER 12

How Do I Protect My Income and Assets?

Insurance is one of the things that we all need and none of us really want. We know it is sensible, but it is just not enjoyable to pay an insurance bill. The main reason for this is that most of the time, nothing goes wrong. We therefore feel that the insurance is unnecessary, and expensive. So often do I hear clients say, "I hate insurance." I never hear this from those that have had a claim.

There are various types of insurance, and the ones that are usually included in a financial plan are the personal (or life) insurances. Interestingly, these are some of the windfall events. There are many millionaires out there who have received a windfall from a claim from a life insurance, trauma, or total and permanent disability policy. Of course, if you have received a benefit from one of these, (including life insurance paid to you under the terminal illness benefit) then you are unlikely to be accepted for more insurance.

If you have a huge windfall, you may not need personal insurances. These insurances protect you so that if something happens to you, then you or your family do not suffer financial hardship. The events which are covered by personal insurances are:

- Death (life insurance)
- Total and permanent disability (Total and permanent disability insurance)
- Major (specified) illness or injury (trauma insurance)
- Disability preventing you from working (income protection and business overheads insurance)

Life insurance   This will be recommended if there is someone who will suffer financial hardship in the event of your death. It is usually a spouse or child who will be disadvantaged, but may also cover anyone else who is financially dependent on you. Life insurance is paid as a lump sum, and can be taken out inside or outside superannuation.

Total and Permanent Disability Insurance (TPD)   This is also a lump sum insurance, and it is paid if you are unlikely to ever work again. Normally, it is available if you are working, and will also cover home duties. A retired person cannot get TPD insurance, nor can anyone with sufficient income to live well on investment income.

Trauma Insurance   As this is a form of insurance which covers specific illnesses and injuries, and is not related to disability, your level of investment income is irrelevant to whether or not this insurance is available to you. The benefit is paid as a lump sum. The conditions covered include but are not limited to:

- Cancer
- Stroke
- Heart attack
- Coronary artery surgery
- Blindness
- Paraplegia
- Severe burns
- Kidney failure
- Major head trauma
- Aortic surgery
- Permanent loss of speech
- Multiple sclerosis

These are indeed traumatic, but not necessarily disabling. I worked with Tom, who, in his twenties required aortic surgery. Once his surgery was over, he was extremely healthy, and only had to give up contact sports. He had no further problems and, because he had trauma insurance, was able to set himself up well with his windfall.

Income Protection and Business Overheads Insurance   These insurances are only available to those who are working, and offer limited benefits if the insured has a significant investment income. These insurances pay a benefit if you are unable to work because of sickness or injury. They will pay monthly after a specified waiting period, and will pay a proportion of your income (income protection) or business expenses (business overheads insurance).

If you have sufficient income and assets that you no longer need to work, then you are unlikely to encounter financial problems because of a change in health, and may not require the above insurances. Your financial planner will advise you as to whether these are appropriate to your financial situation.

General Insurance   Insurance which is not personal is known as general insurance. This includes house and contents, car, health, and a number of other insurances including various business insurances. A general insurance broker can look after all of these for you, or you can go to one of the many insurance providers and arrange it yourself. Brokers are paid commission from the insurance company with whom they place the business, and so will not cost you any extra for their expertise and advice.

Having appropriate insurance in place is essential to effectively managing your windfall. You can follow every instruction in this book, and it may all fall apart without completing this step. Imagine that you have just bought the house of your dreams. It has cost you $2,000,000 of your $4,000,000 windfall. The remaining $2,000,000 has been invested to provide you with a regular income. You don't get around to insuring your new home, and come home one night only to find it engulfed by fire.

What happens next? Well, you will still have the block of land, and that will be worth something, but to replace your house will take most of the remaining cash. You will no longer have sufficient income to support you, so all your good planning has come undone, and you have lost a substantial portion of both your windfall and your income.

Another of the general insurances is travel insurance. It is amazing how often clients tell me that they don't have travel insurance. This doesn't just cover losing your possessions whilst you are traveling. The main purpose of travel insurance is to cover medical expenses if something happens to you whilst you are travelling.

My nieces, Anneke and Monique, recently travelled to Central America. They decided to go on a zip line (flying fox) through the forest as part of their holiday. When Anneke's brake failed, she crashed into a tree, smashing both feet, and breaking her legs, hips, pelvis, and coccyx. This required months of hospitalisation, as well as several operations and two air ambulance flights. The cost of this was around $1,000,000. It is terrible to think what would have happened had she not had insurance.

Both personal and general insurance are important, and it is essential to obtain advice in both of these areas to determine what level of cover is appropriate for you. Your planner/insurance broker will advise you on which insurances you require, and which are unnecessary for you.

SUMMARY

Personal insurances insure you against financial problems caused by changes in health. The types of personal insurances are:

- life insurance
- total and permanent disability insurance
- trauma insurance
- income protection and business overheads insurance

These will not be required if you have sufficient investment income that you no longer need to work.

General insurance covers your possessions and includes house and contents, car, health, travel, and business insurances.

These are essential, regardless of your wealth. You may need the help of a broker to advise you on your general insurance.

In the next chapter, we look at how to ensure that your assets are passed on to your chosen beneficiaries in a tax effective way, once you are not around to supervise the process.

CHAPTER 13

Estate Planning

There is only one real deprivation,
I decided this morning,
and that is not to be able to give one's gifts
to those one loves most.

May Sarton

Earlier in this book, I spoke about having your windfall last a lifetime, and longer. When you have invested and managed your money wisely, you can happily give it all to those you love most, once you no longer need it yourself. Many of you who are reading this book are recipients of someone else's love and generosity, as your windfall has come from an inheritance.

This is the ultimate kindness. To decide that in your lifetime, you, who are the owner and creator of your fortune, will choose not to spend it all, but to keep some aside for those you love. In most cases, because our children are usually middle aged before we close our eyes for the final time, this also means that we are allowing our children time to create their own values and wealth, before we give them the responsibility of managing our wealth, too.

A lot of legal jargon is commonly used when discussing the process of giving to our loved ones (and sometimes strangers) when we die. The document which outlines our wishes is known as a "will" or, in legal terms, "last will and testament." Those who receive a gift from us through our estate are called *"beneficiaries."* All the things that we own that can be passed on to others through a will is known as our "estate." The process of deciding and legally documenting who will receive our money, business assets (if applicable), and personal effects when we die is known as "estate planning."

This is an often overlooked part of planning our wealth. I have met so many parents with dependent children who have not yet made a will. Many of them have substantial assets, and have put off making a will, or updating it to reflect their present circumstances. There are many reasons for this, and probably the most common is a reluctance to really look at the consequences of our own death. It's not a particularly appealing subject. Some clients have expressed frustration at not knowing who to nominate in their will as guardian for their children, and as they have not been able to come to a suitable conclusion, the will has never been completed.

Of course, if you have dependent children, there is an even greater need for a will than if you have no children, or if your children are adults. The reason for this is that if both parents die together (for example, in a car accident) then your precious ones are certainly not in a position to decide what is best for themselves. This decision should be made by those who love them most: their parents.

Estate planning should look at the following things:

- Who are the beneficiaries?
- How much will each beneficiary receive?
- In what form will they receive it?
- When will they receive it?
- What is the most tax efficient method of transferring wealth to the beneficiaries?
- Who do I wish to have as the guardian of my children (if applicable)?
- What happens to my business (if applicable)?
- What assets are included in the will?
- Do I need to create a larger estate to adequately provide for my beneficiaries? (This can be done simply, cheaply, and almost immediately, using life insurance.)

Janne Ashton

This may seem daunting, and certainly is without the help of your professional team. Using an estate planning specialist in a financial planning office, or a solicitor, can make this complex task seem relatively easy. You will need a solicitor to draw up the will and complete the legal processes.

If your estate is complex and involves trusts, self managed super funds, and companies (or some of these), you will need to speak to a specialist. Not all lawyers are specialists, and neither are all financial planners. You will need to ask your financial planner and/or solicitor whether there is a specialist in estate planning in their firm. They will let you know, and may refer you to an associate if they do not have their own expert.

It is important to realise that not all your assets form part of your estate. If you hold something in *"joint tenants"* (that is, jointly held with no separation of the share of ownership), then these assets will automatically transfer to the surviving partner. Assets often held in joint tenants include joint bank accounts, and a family home owned by a married couple. On the death of both parties, it will be dealt with by the estate of the person who is deemed to have died last (if this cannot be determined, as in a plane crash, then it is assumed that the younger person was last to die).

Life insurance may not be dealt with by the estate. If the owner is not the *life insured*, then it will be paid to the policy owner. For example, if Mary owns life insurance on John, then Mary will be paid on John's death, even if she is his estranged ex-wife.

In another example, if the life insured (James) owned the policy, and has nominated a beneficiary (Helen), then the life insurance company is contractually obliged to pay the nominated beneficiary (Helen), so, in each case, the estate is not involved.

You can nominate a beneficiary in your superannuation fund, and this is paid by the trustees of the fund to your beneficiary. You can make a "binding nomination" where the trustees of the super fund must pay the nominated beneficiary. A non-binding nomination is where the trustees have discretion as to whether they pay the nominated beneficiary, or someone else who may have greater need. They can only pay your spouse (includes de facto spouse and interdependency relationship), child (can be adult child), someone who is financially dependent, or your estate. If your estate is paid, then it will deal with your super. If not, then this, too, is outside the estate.

The assets held in companies and family trusts are not included in your estate, as they will continue after your death. All of these assets which are not dealt with by the estate all need to be set up correctly so as to ensure that they go to the correct beneficiary. The shares you hold in the company and your role as controller of the trust may be dealt with by your estate.

The assets which are not part of your estate provide opportunities to have money available to your beneficiaries shortly after your death, without having to wait for the legal process of *probate,* which often takes several months to complete. The other advantage of having assets held this way is that there can be no argument about whether this or that person should be the beneficiary. They must get it, so there is no room for argument (except in the case of a non-binding nomination in superannuation).

SUPERANNUATION AND ESTATE PLANNING

Apart from the advantages mentioned above, superannuation also provides tax effective estate planning. Superannuation can take two forms: lump sum and pension.

Lump Sums If the beneficiary of your estate is considered a "tax dependant," then the lump sum is tax free. The beneficiary must also be a "super dependant," meaning they must qualify as a beneficiary under the superannuation legislation. See table below for categories of dependants.

Janne Ashton

Person	Super Dependent	Pension Dependent	Tax Dependent
Spouse	Yes	Yes	Yes
De facto spouse (includes same sex spouse)	Yes	Yes	Yes
Former spouse	No, unless financially dependent or interdependent	No, unless financially dependent or interdependent	Yes
Child 18 or less	Yes	Yes*	Yes
Child over 18	Yes	No, unless under 25 & financially dependent*	No, unless financial or inter-dependent
Interdependency Relationship	Yes	Yes	Yes
Financial Dependant	Yes	Yes	Yes
Legal Personal Representative (Estate)	Yes	No	No

*Pensions payable to children must be commuted to a lump sum at age 25, discussed further below.

A tax dependant is any one of the following: a spouse, de facto spouse, former spouse (only qualifies as a super dependant if financially dependent or interdependent), child under age 18, a financial dependant, or someone with whom you have an inter-dependency relationship. If the lump sum is paid to a "non tax dependant" (those not listed above), and this includes adult children (18 years and over), then some of it may be taxable. For this reason, lump sums are usually best paid to "tax dependants."

Superannuation Pensions These can only be paid to a "pension dependant" (see table above). Pensions are extremely tax effective, and if either the deceased or the beneficiary is aged 60 or over, then the pension is tax free. Even if both the deceased and the "reversionary beneficiary" (the person who receives the pension from the deceased) are under age 60, there may be a tax free portion to the income, and there will be a 15 percent rebate on any taxable income received.

As an example, if Jack (age 10), receives a pension of $41,000 per annum from his mother, Jill, who died at age 40, how much tax will he pay? We are assuming no tax free portion. It is also important to note that Jack will pay adult tax rates, which are much more generous than child tax rates.

Pension: $41,000
Pension Rebate 15%: $41,000 × 15% = $6,150
Tax on $41,000: $6,150
Tax payable: $6,150 − $6,150 (rebate) = Nil tax payable.

This pension can only continue until Jack turns 25, and then it must be commuted to a tax free lump sum. The example is also relevant for a husband and wife who are both under age 60. Once the reversionary beneficiary turns 60, then it will be tax free.

Testamentary Trusts   A *testamentary trust* is established under a will, and some or all of the assets of the deceased may become the assets of the trust. Testamentary trusts are used for two reasons: tax planning and asset protection.

They may be tax effective, as the trustees can take into account the other income of the beneficiaries, and distribute in the most tax effective manner. One important tax-planning benefit is that income paid from a testamentary trust to a minor is taxed at adult rates. For example, if Bernie dies and leaves his assets in a testamentary trust for his wife, Sarah, and their three children Amy, Beth, and Carey, then they can each receive $6,000 per annum tax free, if they have no other income. So the trustee can distribute $24,000 tax free, and another $116,000 per annum, on which only 15 percent tax is paid. So on a total distribution of $140,000, only $17,400 is paid in tax, leaving over $120,000 for the family expenses.

Of course, both superannuation pensions and testamentary trusts only last while there is still money to distribute. Some testamentary trusts may be set up only to provide income to the beneficiaries, but will eventually have to distribute capital as the trust must be wound up no later than 80 years after it commences.

The other advantage of testamentary trusts is that, as they are not the assets of the beneficiaries, then they cannot be taken by *creditors* in the case of bankruptcy, or an ex-spouse in the case of divorce. The disadvantage with a trust arrangement is that the situation of the beneficiaries may change after the death of the testator (person making the will) and the trust may not have the flexibility to give them the best outcome.

Your estate planning should form part of your financial plan. Even if you have no children or other family, you still will want your estate to go somewhere—a charity, a friend, or a church. My friend Steven used to say that he didn't want to leave his money to his kids (they were not on speaking terms at the time), so he would leave it to a dog's home!

You will need to have an idea of what you want to achieve, and your financial planner or solicitor will work with you to find a workable and tax effective outcome.

SUMMARY

- A will is a document that states where, how, and to whom our assets will be distributed when we pass away.
- Many of our assets are not dealt with by the will.
- A will is important for everyone, and essential for those with dependent children.
- Superannuation provides both opportunities and some traps for estate planning.
- Testamentary trusts may have benefits for tax planning, and also provide advantages in the case of bankruptcy or divorce.

Phase Three:
REVIEW

CHAPTER 14

How Long Will My Financial Plan Last?

I have now taken you through the first two phases of the process, so we now come to the review phase. You can have the best financial plan in the world, and it may not last a year. Why is that? Well, life changes. Your financial plan is a composite of your goals, you current financial position, your choice of investments, your income and expenses, and your estate planning. Because one or more of these can change overnight, your plan needs to be reviewed regularly.

I mentioned before that the best plans are those with built-in flexibility. It is much easier to adjust a flexible plan than to do a complete rework of the plan at a later date. But even the most flexible plans need occasional adjustment.

The review process is built in to your financial planning service. As you go about putting your plan into action, your planner will discuss with you the need for regular reviews. We like to do these at least annually; however, the review process needs to be flexible, as well. If there is any material change to your circumstances, then this will be a trigger for a review.

It is important that you are aware of this, as your financial planner will not know that your circumstances have changed unless you tell him/her. Changes may be subtle, or quite obvious. You may not think that it is relevant at the time, but the following events need to be communicated to your planner so that it can be assessed whether a review is required. The events most likely to trigger a review are:

- Marriage
- Divorce
- Death of a spouse
- Birth of a child
- Any further windfall event
- Changes to your goals
- Change in income
- Change in employment
- Realisation that the plan you have is not working for you in some way
- Major expense not already accounted for in the plan
- Discomfort about performance of your investments
- Long-term or significant change in health
- Decision to move house
- Need for extra funds for investment
- Child/ren leaving home
- Retirement

These will not always require a review, but they are a reason to contact your planner. Many of these are very stressful situations, and will cause emotional as well as financial upheaval. You will need to deal with your emotions all over again, and maybe a completely different set of emotions from those you felt when you first received your windfall.

All periods of extreme emotion involve risk, and you need to take care of yourself during these times. If you need help dealing with emotions, don't be embarrassed to seek professional help from a psychologist or counsellor. Often one session can make a huge difference to how you cope with your emotional response.

The review process is often not as complex as the initial plan. It is a time to adjust the plan to reflect your current situation. The first step is to update your planner on your current situation. If you are due for your annual review (or six monthly: it may be more frequent than annual if you have decided with your planner that this is necessary), then your planner will contact you to arrange the time. You will be asked to provide your planner with updates of any changes to your situation.

Janne Ashton

If the review is a result of an unexpected change in your situation, then it will be up to you to contact and advise your planner of the change. Once the planner has knowledge of any changes to your situation (there may be none), then s/he will set about doing the review.

The review process looks at all aspects of your plan. If there have been changes to your situation, then the plan will need to be adjusted to take these into account. If the changes are major, then you may require a new plan with completely new recommendations. If not, the revised plan will update you on the following:

- Changes to you situation
- Current value of your investments
- Any required changes to strategy
- Performance of the individual investments, and the portfolio as a whole
- Market commentary
- Changes to funds/shares
- Reallocation of money between asset classes
- Changes in fees
- New products
- Legislative changes

Changes to Your Situation   The plan will detail your new situation if this has changed. This provides you with an updated record of your financial position, and provides the basis for the recommendations in the plan.

Current Value of Your Investments   This is actually part of your current situation, and I have listed it separately, as it is probably the change you will be most interested in, and the one which will definitely have changed.

Changes to Strategy   Not every review plan will have strategy changes. These will come about because of a change in your goals, legislation changes or, possibly, your financial position. If there are strategy adjustments, you will need to spend some time discussing these to ensure that the new strategies are exactly what you want.

My clients, Yvette and Patrick, were major lottery winners. They were wise with their money, invested well, and did not overspend. They continued to rent after their win, and some years later advised me that they were purchasing a beautiful house in the country. During their review, I was able to do some strategy planning, which allowed them to keep a comfortable level of income even after purchasing the house, and have some Centrelink age pension support.

Performance of Individual Investments and the Portfolio as a Whole

This part of the plan allows you to measure the performance of your portfolio against expected returns, and compare the performance of individual investments against each other. It also provides a forum for you to discuss with your planner any aspects of your investments that you are unhappy with, or that you particularly enjoy.

Market Commentary   No discussion of investment performance makes any sense without knowledge of the performance of the various markets in which you invest. Market performance is the strongest influence on the performance of your investments. This information in the review is a necessary part of keeping you up to date with the investment landscape.

Changes to Funds/Shares   If there are any investments that your planner feels have underperformed for no apparent reason, s/he may recommend that those investments be sold, or that you reduce your exposure.

Reallocation of Money Between Asset Classes   When there has been significant outperformance (either positive or negative) of one or more asset classes, then your original asset allocation may be out of balance. This will be rectified and brought back into line. The advantage of this is that if, say, Australian shares have fallen in value, then you will buy more while the price is low, and if, say, international shares have risen in value, then you will sell some whilst they are up. This is what we all want to do (buy at the bottom and sell at the top), and this gives us a disciplined way to approximate this strategy.

Changes in Fees and Charges   There may be fees and charges associated with any recommendations which involve changes to your investment portfolio. In this instance, these will be detailed in your review plan.

New Products   Your financial planner will advise you of any new products which have been released in order to help you achieve your desired results. This may mean substituting an old product, or just adding the new product to the mix.

Legislative Changes   These may have a significant impact on the strategy that your planner has recommended, which may result in major changes to the recommendations. There has recently been a reduction in the maximum allowable deductible contribution to superannuation. This has meant that we have had to review our recommendations for many clients.

Your review is an extremely important part of your financial planning. An out of date plan is not only useless, it could be detrimental to your financial future. By reviewing your plan on a regular basis, you will be able to keep on track financially and continue to live life in a way that can only be available to you because of your windfall.

EMOTIONAL RESPONSE TO CHANGES

Your first review is also a time to assess your emotional response. You may well be taking everything in stride, and this may allow you to vary your plan slightly. If you are still ill at ease with your new situation, then this is also relevant. For example, you may still be spending as you did before the windfall, because you fear losing the money. Whilst this will increase your wealth, it may not give you the pleasure that could be yours without risk to your investments. If this is the case, discuss it with your planner, and decide on some treats, so that your day to day spending remains the same, but you plan other expenses that will give you joy.

On the other hand, if you find yourself spending too much, contact your professional team and ask for a review. You will be given options that will allow you to manage your money more effectively. It is really important that you recognise out of control spending, and ask for help. Your professional team is there to help and advise you, not to judge. They will not reprimand or humiliate you; they will just adjust your plan to meet your needs.

SUMMARY

- The review is as important as the initial plan, as it updates your plan as your life changes.
- Reviews should be completed at least annually, or when a change happens in your life, so that the strategy can be adjusted to suit the change.
- Reviews will also update you on how your investments are going and the market factors that are influencing the changes.
- Watch for emotional reactions to either the initial windfall or major changes in your life. Any extreme emotions represent a risk to your financial security, as this is a time when rational decision making is compromised.

CHAPTER 15

Where To From Here?

You now have a wealth of knowledge about the things you need to know so that you can use your windfall to your best advantage. I have covered the following areas:

- The various windfall events
- Emotional effects of a windfall event
- Risks to your wealth
- Dealing with family and friends
- Strategies to minimise risk
- The role of advice in maximising your wealth
- Managing your life budget
- Types of investments
- Choosing a professional team
- Methods of maximising your wealth through tax effective strategies
- Wealth protection
- Passing your windfall on to the next generation

So what more do you need to know? You can always learn more about money. The more you know, the more likely you are to make appropriate decisions. Our website **www.the windfallclub.com.au** is a resource for ongoing support. We will be posting regular updates on the site. These will include the following:

- Education courses for members
- Interest rate updates
- Market updates
- Strategy tips

- Legislative updates for tax and superannuation
- Market commentary
- Links to related sites
- Networking events for members
- Questions and answers
- Testimonials
- Book sales (with a handwritten message from Janne if requested)
- Sourcing of professional team in your area
- Newsletter
- What's new
- Special offers
- Suggestion box

Our website has been designed specifically for windfall recipients. We welcome your suggestions and hope to make it the best resource available for anyone with a windfall.

Take some time to think about and write down what it is that you want from your windfall. Really think about who and what is important to you, as this will make your decisions about money much clearer. For me, this process would involve a short break at a beach somewhere, away from home and the day-to-day activities that occupy our both our time and our thoughts. For you, it may be something completely different. You will need to make sure that you are away from the distractions of day-to-day life. If you have children, do this when they are asleep or with friends. Put your phone on silent and make sure that you do this at a time and place where you will not be interrupted.

Remember that the best way to get maximum pleasure from your windfall is to have it last for the rest of your life. Your professional team will help you to maximise the benefit from your windfall, as that is their job. Be prepared to pay for good advice. Those who try to save a few dollars by not getting advice will almost always be worse off.

On the website, there is a questionnaire to help you when you meet with your financial planner. This checklist is not designed to be comprehensive; it is just a short summary to clarify your goals and the important questions of what and who are important to you. It is good to start thinking about your goals and your core values before you get advice, as this is the basis of all good advice.

I would like to finish by saying thank you for reading my book, and best of luck with your windfall. I hope it brings you everything that you hoped it would and that this book has been of assistance in giving you the education to make your windfall last a lifetime, and longer.

CHAPTER 16

Glossary

Allocated pension: the most common form of superannuation pension, where money is allocated to an account in your name, and you (or on death, your estate) are entitled to all the funds in that account.

Asset class: a broad description of a type of investment. Shares, property and cash are all separate asset classes.

ATO (Australian Tax Office): the government department responsible for tax collection in Australia.

Baby boomer: someone born between 1946 and 1964.

Beneficiaries: those who receive a benefit from you (generally used in connection with estate planning to describe those who receive part of your estate).

Blue chips: shares which are considered the best shares, in that they are strong companies with little likelihood of collapse.

Capital: in investment terms, this refers to the amount of money you have contributed to an investment.

Capital gain: the increase in value of an investment, net of expenses.

Cash: includes a broad range of investments such as "at call" accounts at a bank or other financial institution, term deposits, cash management trusts, and short term money market investments. Cash investments usually have a term of one year or less.

Concessional contributions: contributions to superannuation on which a tax deduction has been claimed; previously known as deductible contributions.

Consumer Price Index (CPI): the measure of inflation which is used in Australia.

Coupon rate: interest rate on a government bond.

Creditor: a lender of money.

Deductible contribution: contributions to superannuation on which a tax deduction has been claimed; now known as concessional contributions.

Diversification: in investment terms, this refers to either investing in different asset classes, or holding a number of different investments within an asset class.

Dividend: income paid by a company to its shareholders.

Estate: your total assets less liabilities at death (net assets) that are passed to beneficiaries through your will.

Estate planning: the process of arranging a will, and planning how to distribute your estate.

Financial institution: a broad term referring to banks, credit unions, building societies, or anyone whose business involves holding money on behalf of others.

Financial plan: is like an instruction book on how to get from where you are now (your current situation) to where you want to be in the future (goals). This is also known as a **statement of advice.**

Financial planner: a professional who uses a broadly based knowledge of finance, and applies this specifically to your own situation to help you achieve your financial and lifestyle goals—also known as a financial adviser.

Financial year: also known as the tax year. In Australia, the financial year is from 1 July to 30 June, and tax is assessed on income (or capital gain) during this period.

Float: the process of listing shares on the sharemarket and bringing them to the public for sale. This can be done prior to listing, and they can be bought from the issuer (the company which is listing).

Fund manager: the institution (or person) who chooses the investments in a managed fund. They are responsible for analysis and selection of investments, and reporting to investors about the return on their investment.

Gearing: investing using borrowed money.

Government bond: fixed interest investment issued by governments when they wish to borrow money.

Growth investments: anything which can grow in capital value over time; usually refers to shares and property.

Hedge: something which provides protection, e.g., an inflation hedge provides protection against inflation.

Illiquid asset: an asset which can not readily or partially be converted to cash, or where you would have to sell at much less than its current value to convert it to cash quickly.

Inflation: an increase in the price of goods and services with no associated improvement in the quantity or quality of the goods or service.

Joint tenants: joint ownership of an asset where there are no distinct shareholdings.

Life insured: a person who has life insurance (not necessarily the owner of the policy).

Listing (or listed): relates to shares which can be traded on the sharemarket.

Liquid asset: an asset which can easily be converted to cash at its current value.

Managed fund: a fund where money from a number of investors is pooled and invested in investments selected by the fund manager.

Market capitalisation: the total market value of a company, calculated by multiplying the number of shares issued by that company by the share price of the company.

Medicare levy: a levy imposed along with income tax, which is used to fund public health care.

Monetary policy: the use by the Reserve Bank of Australia of interest rates to control the demand and the supply of money.

Non-concessional contributions: contributions to superannuation on which no tax deduction has been claimed—previously known as undeducted contributions.

Ordinary: used in financial planning to describe investments or insurance held outside superannuation or pension.

Paraplanners: the people who put together the financial plan and do the research necessary to ensure an appropriate financial plan.

Pay as you go (PAYG): the system of employers deducting income tax from an employee's income, and remitting it to the ATO.

Penny dreadfuls: shares which trade at an extremely low price, are usually illiquid, have small market capitalisation, and have a high risk of failure.

Portfolio: the total of all your investments.

Preservation: a term used to describe the restriction on withdrawal of money from superannuation.

Probate: legal acceptance that a will is valid.

Property securities: property funds which are listed on the stock exchange.

Real: refers to the value of money after taking into account the effects of inflation.

Redundancy: loss of job caused by the position that you hold no longer being required by the employer; also known as bona fide redundancy.

Rent: income return from investing in property. This is paid by the tenants who occupy the property.

Reserve Bank of Australia: the federal government's bank, and the institution which sets and implements monetary policy.

Risk: in financial planning, we describe risk as the possibility of investments falling in value over time.

Risk profile: your personal tolerance to risk.

Salary sacrifice: contributions made to superannuation by your employer from your gross (pre-tax) salary.

Sharemarket: general term used to describe the trading of shares, and their performance, e.g., the sharemarket went up 1% today, or I have money invested in the sharemarket.

Short Term Money Market: where money is traded overnight or for short periods of time. This is used by banks and large companies.

Statement of Advice: another term for a financial plan.

Stock exchange: where shares are traded. In Australia, the main exchange is the Australian Stock Exchange (ASX). There is also the National Stock Exchange (NSX) where you can invest in small companies (very small).

Superannuation: retirement saving in a tax advantaged investment; also known as super.

Tenants in common: ownership of an asset in distinct shares; does not need to be owned in equal shares, and ownership can be transferred (in life or in a will) to a third party.

Term deposit: cash held in a bank for a set term, at a fixed interest rate until expiry of the term.

Testamentary trust: a trust set up in a will for the purpose of holding assets of the estate.

Transaction account: an account with a financial institution which is used for day to day monetary requirements (deposits, withdrawals, paying bills, loan repayments).

Undeducted contributions: contributions to superannuation on which no tax deduction has been claimed; now known as non concessional contributions.

Volatility: the extent of fluctuations in value of an investment.

Windfall: a sudden, large amount of money, which is usually not received as a direct result of actions of the recipient. I have included some windfalls, which are as a result of the recipients' actions, and these include retirement benefits, income for sports people and entertainers, and sale of business.

Special Offer for Readers of *The Windfall Club*

Dear Reader,

As a thank you for reading my first book, *The Windfall Club,* I have written a special report titled "How to protect your windfall when the sharemarket falls." This free report will give you essential information about important benefits available to you during a market downturn:

- A guarantee that protects your windfall from falling in value when the market falls
- No fund manager fees deducted from the guarantee
- No administration fees deducted from the guarantee
- The guarantee locks in rises in value of your investment each year
- Why cash will not protect the value of your windfall over the long term
- A strategy tip that shows you how to potentially benefit from the next downturn

To get your own copy of this free report, please go to **www. thewindfallclub.com.au**.

I hope you enjoy this special report. Thank you again for reading *The Windfall Club*.

Kind regards
Janne Ashton

INVITATION

I invite you to contact me to discuss your financial goals. To contact me, please use one of the following methods:

PHONE: 1300 WINDFALL

FAX: 02 9475 0941

EMAIL: **janne@thewindfallclub.com.au**

MAIL: P. O. BOX 6188
FRENCHS FOREST D.C. NSW 2086